GIVING GOOD GHOST

From the Glossary

St. Martin/St. Maarten—Located about 170 miles from Puerto Rico and lightyears from God, this 35 square-mile island is home to two separate entities, the French Overseas Territory of St. Martin, and the Dutch colony of St. Maarten.

GIVING GOOD GHOST

**Ghost writing:
The St. Maarten entropy diaries—
1994-2000, 25 tall tales;
reprinted columns and essays from
The St. Maarten Guardian, 1995-1999**

Andy Gross

AXUM©

Copyright © 2001 by Andy Gross
All rights reserved.
No part of this publication, except for brief excerpts for purpose of review, may be reproduced, stored in a retrieval system, or transmitted, in any form or by any means, electronic, mechanical, photocopying, recording, or otherwise without the prior written permission of the publisher.

Cover art by Ras Mosera
Cover design By Jenny Li Hellsen

AXUM©
is an imprint of
ELDERBERRY PRESS
1393 Old Homestead Road, Second Floor
Oakland, Oregon 97462—9506

Publisher's Catalog-in-Publication Data
Giving Good Ghost: The St. Maarten
entropy diaries/ Andy Gross
ISBN: 1-930859-01-5
1. Race.
2. The Caribbean.
3. Politics
4. Travel
5. Journalism
I. Title
This book was written, printed, and bound in the United States of America

“Do I dare disturb the universe?”

T.S.Eliot

The author wishes to thank the following for the imaginary bricks needed to complete the perfect Ghost Town:

Ann Barnard
JennyLi Hellsen
Helen and Bernard Kovitz
Ras Mosera
David St.John

While he is at it, the author would like acknowledge the following for their creative influence:

Sherman Alexie
James Baldwin
Jim Carroll
Bob Marley

Recently...

I'm sitting at my brother's table in French Quarter. Mosera is eating an orange, talking about society's rules, and how rigid things are here on St. Maarten. "Man, we have to ignore these laws in order to be real human beings."

I pipe in with this: "there are bigger laws," I say and roll a spoon off of the table and watch it bounce on the tile. "Gravity," I say gravely. "You can't escape it."

The same can be said about St. Maarten. And this too. The universe is expanding, galaxies are flying away from the center with entropic force bound only by infinity. St. Maarten, contrary to the universe, is contracting. Growing smaller and smaller and more self-absorbed until one day soon it will disappear up into its own asshole.

October 1998

"Viruses," Mosera says, "viruses. At night I watch them, the cars, their red taillights going off into different directions scurrying like viruses into holes. That's what's wrong with here. Maybe that's all we are, a whole bunch of viruses and not enough antibodies."

"Looks like what drives me crazy
don't have no effect on you—
But I'm gonna keep at it
Till it drives you crazy, too"
Langston Hughes

It took me a long time to figure out why I found St. Maarten so abusive. I think, more than anything, it's a pervasive sense of entitlement, a baffling sense of inflated self-importance.

Adults acting like terminal adolescents; seemingly sure of what they are doing, yet somehow emotionally arrested and decidedly unsophisticated, distanced from taking responsibility for their actions while expecting others to do the same.

There is no sense of humor, irony, introspection or ambivalence. The only constant is self-promotion.

The pursuit of money, a middle-class life and all its accouterments results in a spirit killing and soul crushing lack of social awareness and sensitivity. There is no room for a serious dialectic, because outside of petty politics, there are no real differences of artistic opinion and appreciation, just an overriding mediocrity.

It's all about what V. S. Naipaul, in a different context, referred to as the enigma of arrival. St. Maarten is so small and fragmented, so twisted by familial alliances and feuds, and so myopic, that issues such as merit and quality never reach the level of importance they should in a developing society.

Its politicians are elected on popularity and the financial favors they can provide. The Daily Herald, the Dutch side's lone newspaper (my beloved Guardian and the Chronicle have folded) regularly prints press releases and one-sided, unattributed stories as news items. Beauty pageant contestants and raffle winners get far more ink than social issues, and the newspaper never misses an opportunity to hype the latest bar, car crash, casino opening or free giveaway at Burger King.

Moreover, it is poorly written, very conservative and pro-Colonial, laughably pretentious, badly edited, and very popular. The public does not demand anything better. You've arrived on St. Maarten just by arriving and naming your hustle. Congrats, there is nowhere to go, or grow.

Antilleans, by that I mean the term used

in St. Maarten to include the residents of the five islands of the Netherlands Antilles, all colonies of Holland, believe anything they create is worthy of being published, recorded or aired on video. It is eerily democratic in its utter lack of discernment or artistic values.

Having an opinion, scheme, a hustle, is not the same as having talent. The sense of entitlement garners the unwavering, unquestioning support of the media in what could best be described as indifferent wonderment.

The work is hailed, the superlatives are hauled out of the dictionaries and self-congratulation abounds. Another masterpiece from St. Maarten. The trick is, it helps to be a St. Maartener. Mosera is a St. Lucian married to St. Martiner. He's the island's best visual artist bar none, and he does receive some acclaim on St. Maarten. But he is not embraced and surely is not celebrated for his achievements, unlike someone like Roland Richardson, who while talented, paints the same flamboyant trees a thousand times over, calls himself a "vessel of beauty," and is neither visionary nor provocative.

It's not just "artists" and politicians. You have people who call in to radio shows and submit viewpoints to the newspapers often beginning their spiels by saying, "I know a lot of you have been waiting for me to comment on this.."

We have?

Early on I bought into this, perhaps because I wanted to fit in and help the cause. Really. But what I found out was that the whole process is vampiristic. It will suck you dry, leave you staggering and waiting for a nice cool coffin to escape to.

They mop up the fawning, undiscerning attention greedily and expect more and more, establishing a precedent for others to come. Mosera, who knows real well what it's like to deal with St. Maarten, said it's as if no one has to pay any dues or develop their art. "They never stop with the mental masturbation," he said.

I often wondered why I cared so much about this and took it so seriously when no one else seems to. Maybe because I sit in this newspaper office like some kind of mollusk letting all of the pollutants travel through me hourly on a daily basis with no place to filter it. Or maybe because I know that really talented people work long and hard, and consider all aspects of their creations before unveiling them, knowing full well that each creative act is a step toward arrival, or perhaps deliverance, and not the thing itself.

Maybe it's because my arrival is stillborn, and being considered a good writer on St. Maarten, or a good anything, is like being called the world's tallest midget. Check it—you are still going to come up short.

Obviously, I'm tired of all this to the point of almost sounding as fucked up as those I criticize.

Sometimes I feel like a raven sitting at the dump picking at a dead dog carcass and saying "never more." But there's always more. Always someone plugging a new CD, diet plan, book of poems.

I once liked it here. My terrible confession. Now I hate it, and it hates me. In a small place, where those native to St. Maarten feel both threatened by and dependent upon the outsiders among them, where secrets, lies, truth and fiction all have equal meaning, there is no room for growth, no time for reflection —everybody is too busy announcing their own premature arrival.

A long time ago, 1994

The clouds above my head are silver and thin and the moon is peeking in, standing on the terrace looking across to the lights of Anguilla. I see my wife of only a few weeks in profile, her hair windswept across her face, looking calm and happy. I'm glad she can live her dream and court the dark Caribbean whenever she wants, worrying only the moon will not be jealous. And I think to myself, just maybe; but I know better.

October 1994

I've been at the Guardian about a year now, and one of my most prolific street sources is a guy named Ronald Peterson. Ronny is from Simpson Bay, which in St. Maarten translates to white, off-white. Ronny is a smart guy, but he says the most outrageous things. For instance, he told me today he fought with the Israeli army during the six-day war in 1967. He speaks some Hebrew, but this seems far-fetched. Jenny Li , who lived in Israel for almost nine years, says the Israeli army would never trust a non-Jew or non-Israeli enough to take them in the army.

Ronny, through his family, is pretty close to Claude Wathey, St. Maarten's long time ruling boss. Because of this Ronny thinks he has all kinds of inside information, and some of it is probably valid and newsworthy. Trouble is, Ronny adds this conspiratorial, spy novel twist to it, so even the simplest tip he gives me is riddled with incredible intrigue and reminders such as, "this is so hot, it will blow the lid off of St. Maarten. They (he never says who) are ready to put a stick up DR's ass. Just don't use my name."

Ronny drops very broad sotto voce hints that he is tied in with the local Chinese mafia and smuggles Chinese nationals to American soil in the Virgin Islands. He's a bit coy on this point, and if he does it, it's probably for the money, because Ronny, for all his 'bawn-here' blood, his intelligence and his ambition, can't hook up with a decent job. What I like about Ronny is that his whole trip, though nutty, is creative and fueled by his wanting to be more than he is. I certainly can relate.

Past midnight

You and me
my imaginary companion
driving in pre-dawn darkness
past
sinister fields where not even crows stir
spaces where UFOs could land and lift off
unnoticed, except by us
their glow the unearthly light in front of us
an illumination:
your white fingers
tracing the glowing radio stations of infinity

January, 1999

Went to New York to avoid spending New Years in St. Maarten. All in all, a good move. After farewells, I get in this taxi to take me from my parents' apartment to JFK and give the driver a cursory "how are you doing?" He asks me if I really care. I shrug and tell him I was just taking a shot at being friendly to see if I still had it in me. Evidently I don't.

He looks me up and down and says, "you look like a rabbi with a drug problem."

Now, this could be considered insulting, but I find it kind of charming, flattering even.

Maybe accurate as well. Though I don't tend to practice it myself, I like honesty, especially when it's loopy.

"If you have a problem with drugs, it's OK with me," he says. I nod and say nothing. But enough about me. He's ready to change gears.

He begins confiding in me, maybe as if I am a rabbi. "I just lost my best friend," he says. "He was only seven, and boy, how he suffered. Do you want to see his picture," he asks.

I don't, especially if it's some poor little kid who's been wasted by cancer or one of those diseases they're always holding telethons for. He turns around and pulls out his wallet and unfolds a series of seven or eight photos, not of a kid, but of a Rottweiler, including one of the dog in a sawed-off charcoal tuxedo. He's telling me about the dog, looking over his shoulder, one hand on the wheel while going 60 mph, unsuccessfully trying to fight back tears.

Seems his daughter, the only good thing that ever happened to him, just got married, and he had a tuxedo made for the dog, whose name was Oscar. Oscar was too sick to go to the wedding service and reception so he had the dog photographed wearing the custom-made tux as a keepsake.

There's not much I can add at this point, as I listen to the guy tell me about the thousands of dollars he's spent on veterinarian bills and experimental medicines.

He asks me what I do in St. Maarten. I tell him I'm a professional hate object. He either does not hear me, or ignores it. He says he'd like to go to a place like St. Maarten or Aruba and make a killing, financially speaking.

"Oh man, you could have it made there. It's warm all the time, no hassles, no restrictions," he tells me.

"In a place like that, a smart guy like you or me could have real power, real power," he says, pulling into the exit where a family of 12 tearfully say frantic goodbyes in Spanish amidst boom boxes, strollers, suitcases and what looks to me like a refrigerator.

The ride is over and the fare is $35. I fish around in my pants and give him a $50 because despite the whole sad story and risky driving, I actually enjoyed the trip.

He thanks me and gives me a big smile, tells me once again it's OK if I'm on drugs, because "you seem like a nice guy."

Then, almost as an afterthought he brightens and tells me, "Hey, if you ever need a partner down there, we could really take over,"leaving me to wonder how he got to "we."

"Sorry about the dog," I tell him and walk into American Airlines for one last flight to St. Maarten, the image of a Rottweiler in a tux sitting in a synagogue full of semi-pious rich congregants led by a rabbi with drug problems fueling me past swarming skycaps.

What I did on vacation

The city of your birth chases you like a crazy woman
swinging a frying pan while wearing an apron and nothing else
strings flowing behind her;
you cling and she laughs
you approach and she blushes
uses that pan like a fan
demure, she coils herself and
swings her breasts
the promise of succulent geometry drawing you in
hungry fool, lips empty
she smiles at the cast iron irony; she swings, you miss
then chases you through unformed streets

leapfrogging urine-soaked men
who hug sidewalks
and murmur I love you to memorized mer-
maids that have crawled out of methadone
dreams
careening past leaning Chinese gathered
around a meat grinder watching tomorrow's
dim sum dumplings come pumping out of a
pork primer like beads on an abacus
looking at you like lunch;
Hurriedly you hurdle Hasidim who dangle
diamonds and hide scrolls in their curls, so
covetous of carats-
Patiently, she waits
watches while you dip down into the subways
and ride trains
safely but unsatisfying transported like a
parasite in a steel stomach
glance at the red lips and blue finger nails of
her newest recruits
count the nails in your coffin and squint
when skylight reappears and she's waiting for
you
ready to go loping over hypnotic bridges
high above the river my father swam when
he was a boy
long past currents,
spying a bar graph of a city sitting like a prize
in a Cracker Jack box

you stand stunned at the weight of your own
longing
she yawns
and breaks your heart
opens the beating envelope of your desire and
licking it,
stamping expectantly, she's cornered you
"will she kill me," or "will I jump," you ask.
But she
tilts her head
and brushes you with her hair
crying terminal tears
even as she leads you back
your fingers knotted in her strings
pan in hand, the clanging of the clinging
against your smacked soul the only accom-
paniment.

In A Case Like This, What Then Must We Do? Reprinted from the St. Maarten Guardian, March 3, 1998

Maybe your day, maybe your life is like this. You wake up, and inside you feel split in countless parts, splintered. You spend a good deal of your time refereeing the disputes in your own head that only you are in tune to, as if plugged into some private radio station in Hell.

You wander around, annoy and scare people; scrounge money where you can. You walk, ragged, often barefoot. Your drug consumption like the other details in your life, is hazy, but consistent.

You act crazy, and maybe you are; but not so crazy you don't hear them laugh, don't hear them whisper about you, wax lurid about what you did, about who you are. That you killed your father because he was abusing you, abusing your mother.

You snapped like dry kindling.

You cry and say you begin to believe you were born a dead man.

Maybe your day ends like this.

You have a house but Hurricane Luis kissed your roof good bye.

You sleep here and there, the sky above you, crouching, waiting to reclaim you. You hear your own breathing, a sound like a shovel sinking into warm soil.

Maybe your life is like this.Chances are it is not.But until last Friday, this was Roy Cannegieter's life, or more precisely, this was what Roy's life seemed to be, because in many ways, the mentally ill, like the truly gifted, are unknowable.

Getting at their essence is like peeling an

onion; the layers peel off and off and off, and there is a core, and unless you are careful, and maintain distance, it can bring you to tears. Roy is gone now. He was sent to the Capriles Clinic in Curacao late last week.

It is not the first time he's been in a psychiatric facility. In recent months, Roy had found some solace and medical attention with Dr. Michael Mercuur and his staff who ostensibly treated him quite well and without charge.

Patient confidentiality being what it is, it will never be clear if Roy was committed by Mercuur or whether the decision was Roy's, or a mutual one. Ultimately, the distinction is unimportant. Shortly before he was scheduled to leave, Roy, though anxious about what lay ahead, also seemed relieved; he knew at some level that living on the streets was eventually going to shorten his already hard life. Roy is 42, but looks older. He's been in jail several times. He walks stiffly, with a jerky gait because his body has gone rigid, an indication of some kind of arthritic internal rebellion and self imprisonment. Years of neglect have taken their toll; at least 24 of Roy's teeth are gone, and he suffers from constant sores and rashes due to bathing primarily in seawater.

I have known Roy for four years and realized quite early on that there was simply no place for him on St. Maarten. Roy had not merely slipped through the cracks and safety nets of family, Antillean social security and community, he had become an embarrassment, a sometimes criminal, a pariah, and finally, invisible, a non-person to many.

That Roy is again in a psychiatric facility is an anti-climax. The truth is, he should have been in some kind of structured environment a long time ago, and not left to fend for himself on the streets.

In some ways, Roy, in his clear need of treatment, presented a challenge to the community that was largely unmet.

But Roy's luck in general was never particularly good. A case in point. Roy was released from one of his jail terms the day *before* Hurricane Luis in 1995. An orphan in the storm, he lost his roof and despite his attempts to buttonhole anyone in government who might listen, it was never replaced. Months later, he was in jail again.

I do not believe any governmental office ever helped him in a meaningful way, though certain individuals did treat him kindly. Not that Roy was that easy to help. He could be manipulative and canny, a hustler at heart.

Add to that stubborn and demanding. Also, to say Roy has a dark side is a bit like saying the ocean has water. But that aside, Roy is a human being who deserves a life with some comfort and dignity. A life that was denied him on the streets. In the coming years, there will be more cases like Roy, though perhaps not as deeply rooted in violence and familial shame, and St. Maarten will have to address the problem of mental illness and homelessness in a humane, logical and therapeutic manner.

Schizophrenia, psychosis and depression will have to be treated the same way diabetes, asthma and anemia are treated — illnesses that require treatment, medication and aftercare, and not as afflictions that are stigmatized and steeped in shame and isolation. It will be a challenge, to be sure.

In the mid 19th century, the great Russian writer Leo Tolstoy used to walk the streets of Moscow and St. Petersburg troubled by the condition of the poor and mentally ill. He realized that even if he gave each poor and sick person a few rubles it would not change things. He was left to ruminate on a variation of the Biblical quandary, "am I my brother's keeper?" It led him to ask the question, "what then must we do?"

His eventual answer was a kind of pure Christian spirituality untainted by organized religion and persecution. Tolstoy figured each individual had to add his or her own "light" to the "son of light" in order to create revolutionary social changes.

It might come as a surprise, but Roy is religious. He's looking for something. Perhaps it is forgiveness, or the serenity to forgive himself.

A while ago, out of some intrusive nowhere, I asked him if it was true he killed his father. He looked at me, decidedly steady and sane, and said, "no more than he killed me."

Take care Roy.

Gunga Din drops his bucket

I honestly feel like an ass for writing so much about independence for St. Maarten in the Guardian. I feel like Gunga Din carrying water for someone else while going thirsty all the while.

Little good it's done except to make me feel like a third-class citizen in alien space, advancing a cause I could never be a part of and most importantly, a cause neither Lasana Sekou or others seem willing to bring to the fore. I have to admit that at times I feel sorry for Sekou and his brother Jose Lake Jr., because getting the message out in St. Maarten, overcoming that kind of apathy is almost impossible.

I respect Sekou's intelligence and grasp of history; his sense of place. But I have my problems with him, and I've never been able to reconcile them in my own head.

Maybe it's that "bawn-here" thing. I never felt Sekou was comfortable having non-Antilleans as exemplars on St. Maarten, be they white or from other Caribbean islands like my friend Mosera. The whole concept is a type of St. Maarten nationalism, which when you look at it, is ridiculous. A vast majority of people living on the island are from somewhere else, with the number of indigenous, "bawn-heres" ever dwindling. Contributions to the St. Maarten/"bawn here" cause were always accepted, but inclusion was never part of the deal.

Sekou always gave the impression he needed to be directing things, appropriating them for his vision for St. Maarten.

As a publisher, his reach extends far enough to include such Caribbean men of letters as George Lamming and Edward Brathwaite, and this does give him some luster.

I think I'd respect him more as a person and writer if he had a sense of humor or sense of irony, or, if he treated me in a way that did not make me feel like a butler, taking a soft cloth to put the fake shine on his Las Vegas by-the-sea of an island.

Sekou, born Harold Lake, is the number one St. Maarten nationalist. He is a publisher and a writer of accomplishment; ambitious and teleological. I always likened him to a clock where you can watch all the intricate parts moving with precision, mechanical cunning and elegance, but no emotion.

His rhetorical and polemical stance has long been independence for St. Maarten. His rhetoric, while not racist per se, always skirts the fine line of ennobling Afro-Caribbeans at the expense of whites, though Sekou himself has benefited greatly from the largess and kindness of non-Caribbean people like Blanca Hodge, the head of the Philipsburg Library.

Many of his House of Nehesi projects are funded through grants made possible by Dutch auspices. Unlike other publishers, House of Nehesi risks little or none of its money on projects. Sekou is equally comfortable taking money tarnished by colonialism as he is protesting the colonialism itself.

As local revolutionary in residence, he assumes the mantle of rebellion without any of the risks and all of the paradoxes.

When Queen Beatrix visited St. Maarten, none other than Sekou, and my former boss and anti colonialist Fabian Badejo, were contacted by yet another corrupt edition of the Island Government to chair a committee to welcome her. Nothing against the queen, but if you are an independista, a nationalist, or even vaguely cognizant of what you are doing, there is no way you'd agree to take on such a task. This type of dissonance by Sekou and Badejo is illustrative of a lot of what goes on on St. Maarten—somebody advocating one position, then abandoning it for a few bucks, a political favor, the possibility of getting laid, or just 15 minutes of fame on the radio.

Back to royalty. Sekou had the idea of commissioning a portrait of the queen. Mosera told me he was approached about it. I told him he'd be crazy to do it, even if the money were decent, unless he did a Salvador Dali or Pablo Picasso variation and painted the queen with two heads, three tits and no throne. Given Sekou's preachings on the subject of colonialism, it would have been more telling if he had organized a rally at which pretty Queen B's portrait was burned in effigy.

Sekou, who holds a Dutch passport and preaches independence, has yet to lead a single act of civil disobedience, save for an in-house "shout down" against the Franco Dutch Treaty; or to protest any of the multitude of injustices on the island which range from bad roads and utilities to racism, classicism and homophobia to an HIV epidemic, to the ever-popular political and judicial corruption.

He reportedly took a consultant's fee to organize an "artistic" tribute to welcome his queen. It's similar to when he went to work as the interim head of the Government Information Services knowing full well his political agenda did not meet that of his employers. Likely he did it to benefit House of Nehesi Publishing contacts. It's all so very St. Maarten.

One House of Nehesi project he took on was a series of motivational, trite homilies-for-success done by a husband and wife team I long suspected were into partner swapping, S & M, and bird watching, and not in that order.

It's incongruous to think that this shit is published by the same entity that gained the trust of the venerable Barbadian novelist

George Lamming, an author many felt should have been the Caribbean's first Nobel Prize winner in literature, instead of the St. Lucian-born Derek Walcott.

For better or worse, Sekou has made book publishing a far more democratic and accessible, albeit mercenary goal on St. Maarten than ever before. The only question is, at what price quality?

Polite

Your talking of shackles raises my hackles
you live off the Love Boat, not some slave tote
if it weren't so trite
it might be dire
call me a liar
anywhere else
you're just low flyers crashing into high tension wires
pocket revolutionaries with government jobs
can't drop bombs
lest you lose your perks
well fed, inbred
no sense of dread
no liquid irony
a branch on the family tree

sterile leaves
incestuous buds
bark grown dull
what you need is a flood
a modern day Noah
won't say yo yah
fuck up your ark
my bite is my bark
Bawnhere
crying so much about the Dutch mama
you love the umbilical noose
can't set yourself loose
led around by your dick
you turn the trick
circus monkey jumpin'
through hoops of green lumpy
cash on the ass
Bawnhere
casino girls light skinned humpin'
throw in your poker chips
freedom in chits
bullshit
send away for pimp kits
learn to look everywhere for tits
bawnhere
no rude boy just crude boy
stay nothing but lewd boy,
never grow up to be men
don't know when to say when

Nothing subtle in your rebuttal
make me a white guilt lackey
what if I call you blacky?
Racism on a one way street
expect me to bleat like a sheep?
White meat dark meat
KFC is a god
the church is Prozac
another kind of blackjack
dealing from the bottom of a colonized pack
I'm a poet
I know it
hope I blow it
Mr. Chairman in the box,
all so polite and uptight
good afternoon good evening good morning
good night good evening good day good night
Where's my manners?
Lost in the meeting of Black business plan-
ners
Listen for a second and just sit tight-
did I get the order right?
Should I put a comma here and there to be
polite?
Motherfuck all of you to death, and good
night.

Stimulating a gentile
September 1998

Contrary to popular belief, I actually have a day job. Yup, I wait for strange people to come into the august offices of the St. Maarten Guardian and give me news. Never mind that I used to go out and try to get it, the news. But after a time of humping it, of going into the community and getting stories, and then realizing nothing could or would ever change on the friendly island, I just got discouraged. Or maybe I just learned the cold fact that I would have no impact, no voice, no matter what. I learned my lesson after I chased down a story about a Haitian woman who passed away at age 28. I got the information from a police report and followed up. I wondered what happened to her.

It turns out she had been sick, but was on the island illegally and could not seek medical attention. My snooping around resulted only in her body being held by the medical examiner for four days pending an autopsy, which revealed she died of natural causes.

No meaningful journalistic exposé on the lack of access to healthcare, no response from officials, no nothing, except her next of kin had to wait longer for her body.

I found out where she had been living and went there. Inside the small house on Mt. William Hill, a young man held the passport picture of the woman in his hands and looked at me with a half-smile; looking at me from far away as a sad bolero played in the background.

Then there was the sad case of Karen, who once taught dance at the cultural center on Backstreet, but fell in love and into trouble with drugs and wound up fatally stabbed in some Backstreet alley. Despite her drug use history, friends were quick to say she was clean. I remember the public prosecutor kept her body for a long time because it was a murder case and there were clues and evidence to be gleaned. I remember her father, the golf playing accountant who always wore his ties flapped over rather than knotted, coming into the Guardian, just as he had gone into all the other media outlets to state his case that the body be released.

I don't remember him looking stricken or in mourning or anything like that. He looked pissed off, like someone caught in traffic who was in danger of missing his tee time at the Mullet Bay golf course.

I thought this is a guy who probably didn't

even remember what his daughter looked like as a child, couldn't remember a single Father's Day gift she'd given him, probably didn't know she enjoyed dancing. What I do recall was that he was cracking his gum quickly and noisily like a Geiger counter gone mad in a room full of uranium. "We want her body back," he said. " We want to be finished with this." He sounded embarrassed and he never mentioned a word about loving or missing his dead daughter.

After these types of things and more, I thought it better to conserve my energy and sanity, though both are in short supply.

Anyway, one day, a woman comes in and says she "wants to make a report" which to me always sounded more like a police matter. She said her 12-year-old son was suspended from Our Lady of Perpetual Motion School, or some other Catholic institution of lower learning because, in her words, "he was stimulating a gentile."

"What," I asked.

"You know," she says, and then she moves her hand to near her crotch and makes a circular motion.

It strikes me the lady might be crazy, but then I realize what she's trying to say.

"Oh," I say, 'you mean he was stimulating his genitals."

"Right." she says beaming, happy we've had this breakthrough.

Then she asks, "is that a good thing?"

Jose Lake Jr.'s Rope-a-Dope With Boycott Opponents
Reprinted from the St. Maarten Guardian, December 17, 1997

Freedom fighters don't get much rest, let alone time to skim a magazine. There was Joe Lake Jr. standing quietly Friday morning at the Paper Garden leafing thorough some magazine, maybe People, maybe Ebony, definitely not Colonial Digest, when he ran into Steve Lake.

What followed was an impromptu debate on Joe Lake's campaign to boycott the upcoming Parliamentary Elections. Steve Lake, though friendly and funny, is as excitable and loud as Junior Lake is measured. So, there was Steve Lake telling Junior that he was wrong, that you have to vote to change things and that you can't waste a vote.

And there was Junior, dark sad eyes and all, but smiling that beatific little smile he smiles when he's talking the politics of freedom, smiling ever so slightly, like a surgeon about to perform a colonial-ectomy.

A woman of Hispanic descent wanders by and asks the Paper Garden staff about sympathy cards in Spanish. Maybe it was for the death of Option A. She looks confused. The Lakes smile at her and get back to brass tacks. They continue their debate, and in the spirit of the conversation if not verbatim reportage goes on like this:

Is not voting like wasting your choice to change things? Isn't voting for any of the existing politicians the same thing? They are toy soldiers. They can affect no change in a system geared toward their continued subjugation and impotence. Let us go the route of Aruba. What if the requirements of the Treaty of Maastricht make that an impossibility? Didn't the SPA boycott the elections in 1979?

Junior and Steve go outside and the discussion continues on the steps of the Paper Garden as the sun climbs a step-ladder in the sky spreading little diamonds across each Lake's pate. Junior is like Muhammad Ali versus George Foreman in the "rumble in the Jungle." He's using the rope-a-dope, no offense Steve, letting his opponent use up energy, while he balances against the ropes, popping forth with enough brief rallies to keep things interesting.

A passerby tells the verbally excitable Steve Lake to watch his blood pressure. Steve Lake says that's why he takes garlic. The passerby digests that one. Somehow it all makes sense. Then it's over, if not resolved. Steve Lake says goodbye and Junior Lake is smiling that little smile.

It turns out Lake vs. Lake was just a preliminary bout.

We also had Commissioner Julian Rollocks saying Junior's call for a boycott was irresponsible. Rollocks argued that with Afro-Caribbean people, especially women, having struggled so mightily for the right to vote, Lake's call was inexcusable.

Rollocks, like others, has said Lake should have formed a list and contested the elections to prove his point. Others have said Lake is using this as a subterfuge to push even harder for independence.

The missing link here is that freedom and political independence are not ideas to be defended, especially in an arena as tainted, undemocratic and dysfunctional in nature as the electoral system currently in place in the Netherlands Antilles.

Independence is a natural process, organic

and intrinsically undefinable. It is what it is; the ocean is not asked to prove it swirls from Africa to the Americas; the moon does not need a letter of reference from the sun; a river does not have to justify itself.

Lake understands this, and as the voices against the boycott continue and grow more panicky and paranoid—witness Louis Laveist's latest take on Lake—the calm rope-a-dope will continue.

Tuesday, Laveist, a Democratic party candidate, posited his conspiracy theory that Lake was being used by the St. Maarten Patriotic Alliance (SPA) to ensure they stayed in power. What was not said by Laveist was that perhaps Lake was being paid by the SPA to promote a boycott.

Ah, yes. Of course. And Junior is next in line to become Pope and also knows why the U.S. Government is suppressing evidence on alien visitations and proof that Michael Bolton is the antichrist.

Later Tuesday afternoon, and Lake is standing in front of the Newsday offices with Scottie Priest and Hondo Rami. Priest has eyes that issue challenges; Rami looks on.

Laveist's comments and intimations of SPA payoffs are mentioned. Lake shakes his head and smiles, amused that people might actually think the SPA is paying him. Someone says Laveist said what he said for purely political reasons. That he has no idea what the boycott means, and what a travesty the system is.

Lake considers this, nods patiently at the obviousness of it all.

Head tilted slightly, dark eyes on the prize; Junior Lake smiles that smile, and bends a bit into the ropes as blows, real and imaginary, whistle past him like ghosts in a graveyard.

System shutdown
January 1998

More and more these days, I feel myself retreating deeper and deeper into my no exit zones. I've shut off so many parts of me, I only have to pay a skeleton crew to run my day-to-day operations, if you know what I mean. But every once in a while, something sneaks up on me, a yearning, a remembrance of exuberance and unfettered joyfulness. Today I heard the song "Just Got Lucky," by the JoBoxers and flashed back to 1983 in some sort of transcendent reverie that reminded me, however painfully, that I was once someone else.

February 1998

Big doings here in Zombieland. Linda Badejo-Richardson, the ex-wife of my boss Fabian, has cooked up this scheme to sell special sunglasses so residents of St. Maarten can view the "partial total eclipse of the sun". Partial total is like the old cliche of being half pregnant. It's either total or not. Like 91 percent is not the same as 100 percent. It's total in Guadeloupe and Aruba, not in St. Maarten. This isn't deterring Linda as she hawks the product like the Amway representative she always will be, calling it the "last chance to see the last partial total eclipse" of this century. Whew. She's even created her own company, Global Contact, to get the message out. She's running a real scare campaign on this, bringing in some eye doctors from Curaçao to tell St. Maarteners how dangerous it is to look at the eclipse without shades. Telling everyone how the sun will go gangster on their retinas. Hey, if that's the case and we have all these newly blind people walking around stumbling into tourists, maybe we can put all the poor stray dogs to work as seeing eye mutts.

Linda has donated some shades to school children so in some ways, this is a valuable public service, I guess. But she's created so much hype with all this stuff that people are bound to be let down when there's no darkness at noon. True to form, the next day, the Guardian's main competitor, the Herald ran a headline that said, "Partial total eclipse a disappointment."

Actually, it was kind of nice. It got a bit dark and cooler, like it was 5 p.m. instead of 1 p.m. and the shadows had this long, velvety quality like they were painted on the streets; sort of an angelic fingerpainting.

Using the shades, I looked at the sun and saw the moon stealing across like a lover sneaking out the door before things got too hot.

I bet Linda must have ordered 5000 pairs of those eclipse shades at about $2 a pop from some factory in China and maybe sold 100 at $6. She didn't figure that most very frugal St. Maarteners would simply share one pair of these miracle shades among groups of 20 or 30, or your average nuclear family of Arrindells, Richardsons, or Hodges. I half expected Roy to stumble in half-blind from staring at the sun and thinking he'd seen Jesus or Elvis, or portents of the end of the world, but he told me later he slept through the whole thing. I bet he was just fine with a nice mixture of thorazine and superduper Valium he gets from a doctor on Backstreet and whatever else he scrounges up. The only one who went out of control was the woman who stands at the Food Center roundabout holding a placard warning that the end, as we all know, is near. Reportedly she fainted in the middle of the road and narrowly missed being run over in the time it took someone to say "get out of the street you psycho."

My wife put a pair of the shades on our big dog Aramis, and he looked great. In fact, he may have started a new fashion trend. I saw a basset hound trotting down Frontstreet wearing a pair, and he too, looked smashing. The partial total eclipse lasted about 90 minutes and ended 3:30 or so. At 3:35 Linda announced a 50 percent off sale on all eclipse viewers.

October 1997

My boss Fabian is spending a lot of time promoting Fernando Clark, an aspiring stand-up comic. Fernando's main obstacle is that he's not all that funny in a universal way. He can be funny at times, but basically his humor is too provincial, too dependent on local inside jokes, references and insults, to make him anything more than a St. Maarten celebrity.

Also, when Fernando takes the stage, his humor can be brutal and insulting; not satirical, but sledgehammer blunt.

The Guardian was helping to promote his comedy show at a local hotel and Fabian asked me to interview Fernando. I gladly did so, because I think he's a smart guy, with a conscience. He has good powers of observation, that unfortunately don't always make it into his jokes, maybe because he knows being sly and subtle won't work in St. Maarten, or, because he is incapable of it in his own right. During the interview, I asked Fernando if he believed that most funny people were either depressed and angry at heart, or some combination of both, and that's what fed their humor, their need to turn the joke around on someone else.

He said he felt neither of those things. "How could I be unhappy and make people laugh," he asked me. Which showed me he wasn't connected to the rabid word slinger who took to the stage like it was a street fight.

I'm not sure if the adage about comics being unhappy people is axiomatic, but I think people who try to be humorous in a public forum, whether it be on stage, or like myself, in print (though I'm sure most of my "readers" would debate whether I'm funny or not, which means of course, the joke would be on me), are generally seeking to right (or write) emotional wrongs in a solipsistic and childlike way, or to compensate for some kind of lasting internal pain that can only be assuaged temporarily and absurdly by humor.

August 1998

It's sad to see what's happening to the island. Before the big cruise ships, before the killer hurricanes, before the island was given away like a dowry to rich suitors, it must have been so magical here. It's still really beautiful in green Colombier, huddled underneath Pic Paradis, surrounded by verdant fields with grazing cows and tall weeds blowing in the wind. The island is still dramatic elsewhere, with its mountains and fantastic sweeping views of the sea and the Caribbean, always glittering.

But the island is being raped. Literally.

Earth movers take huge chunks out of hillsides, while greedy Americans, Europeans and St. Maarteners build on every last acre of land. The ponds are being ruined, wildlife is disappearing, and the once beautiful beaches are not quite so beautiful anymore. The island is turning into one large ashtray, one large dumpster, overflowing at that.

St. Maarten is traffic clogged with too many cars and too many people who disrespect the island's beauty by throwing garbage out on to the roads, or by pumping waste into the sea and ponds. It is scarred by others who regularly circumvent regulations and put large, nondescript buildings virtually anywhere they like, without proper infrastructure, which means more sewage seeping onto roads, more garbage that cannot be safely disposed of, and more clutter.

A few years ago the island still had the whiff of salt spray mixed with airconditioning condensation. Now it smells like Chinese food mixed with smoke.

I bet older people like Rosa Guy and Beryl Parker Hazel who knew what it was like a long time ago, and young people like Esther Gumbs who listen to the land, can actually hear it weep from sheer violation. I wonder if it is possible for an island to sink into the sea from the weight of its own unhappiness and the knowledge of its imminent destruction.

The Amplified Music of Independence Reprinted from the St. Maarten Guardian, March 17, 1998

The music of independence goes like this, a few random, tentative notes, someone trying out a melody. Then, others join in, their notes united by a percussive beat, an insistent drummer, music that grows stronger and stronger, a life unto itself.

Lately, a number of factors have led to that music being amplified.

First, there was the survey results Friday that indicated 15 percent of St. Maarteners favored independence. Then, there was the 11th hour flailing and eventual rejection Monday by the Executive Council (EXCO) of the externally imposed Franco-Dutch Treaty. Add to that the failure of any of the political parties on the Federal level to find enough common ground to form a government, a likely sign of a moribund Netherlands Antilles.

And finally, or more precisely, continuously, there is Jose Lake Jr., who has had the music of independence humming in his head for a long time, watching quietly in the wings, waiting, the avatars perched on his shoulders.

Despite the opinions of "the experts" who say otherwise, the results of a survey that determined 15 percent of St. Maarteners favored independence is certainly significant. For one, it represents a huge increase over the six percent who voted for the independence option in the 1994 constitutional referendum, and it certainly represents a greater segment of the voting population than the Serious Alternative Peoples Party (SAPP)-Elton Jones mini-coalition can claim at the moment.

For another, what is unsaid is the growing number of St. Maarteners between the ages of 16 to 25 who have yet to exercise their political power in any way but who anecdotally constitute a potentially huge pro-independence voting block.

These are young people who see neither passion nor any potential for progressive politics in the current political system; young people for the most part who are too hip, too smart and too schooled in the language of ironic protest to be morally comfortable aligning themselves with the sour status quo. No Willie Lynch for them.

Which brings us back to Lake. Almost single-handedly he has fought the Franco-Dutch Treaty and essentially shamed the island Council into rejecting the treaty. Indeed, the specter of Lake and independence hovered over the Island Council's decision. If not for Lake and his outspoken pressure, who knows what might have happened.

Almost four years ago, Lake, his dark eyes blazing, likened independence to a "wind that builds in Africa, picks up speed over the Atlantic and blows the colonial fortress down." The winds blowing as they are, sooner or later, Lake is going to have to make a decision about forming an Independence Party to contest next year's Island Council elections. So far, he has not made the decision, for a lot of understandable reasons.

Lake, the president of the Independence for St. Maarten Foundation is a humanist and activist, not a politician. He would likely not cut the kind of deals that are part of the political currency, nor would he be inclined to utter meaningless platitudes and empty promises. Add to that list the matter of money. It takes a lot of cash to run an effective campaign these days.

There are other reasons. Lake is too introspective, too self-critical, too much a loner to be a politician in the conventional sense. You can see it in the way he deflects praise, refuses to be pigeon-holed as a leader. In short, unlike the current elected politicians, he is less "ham," than he is Hamlet, the troubled and self-doubting Shakespearian hero.

In one way or another, fathers haunt sons. That is not all of course, but it is there. For some sons, it may be the burden of finishing their father's work, of advancing a legacy that is both your birthright and your destiny. Junior is the son of Joseph Husurrell Lake Sr., publisher, freedom fighter, trade union activist and Caribbean integrationist, who died in 1976, broken, but unbowed.

Joe Lake Sr. did not have an easy time. According to information presented in National Symbols, a book edited and compiled by Joe Lake's Sr. son Lasana Sekou, his father faced ostracism and vilification.

In the 1960's, people had to hide in alleys in order to read Lake Sr.'s dissident and seminal Windward Islands Opinion, lest someone from the ruling government of Claude Wathey find out. Lake Sr. was spat upon, threatened and ultimately died of troubling, somewhat mysterious causes at the age of 50.

Perhaps as one of Junior's best friends pointed out, "maybe he thinks about what happened to his father and has second thoughts. Junior is exactly the same age his father was when he died. Maybe he thinks, 'what if I do it and fail, then what?"

But there is the matter of destiny. The real political legacy of St. Maarten is not that of the late Claude Wathey and crippling partisan politics played for profit on a colonial craps table, but that of the unfinished agenda of Lake Sr. and the larger vision of Caribbean integration shared by his sons.

If and when it happens, that an Independence Party is formed, Lake will have to articulate how St. Maarten will feed, govern, protect and provide health care for itself as an independent nation.

Lake will have to provide a logical blueprint to those who are visionary-impaired in order to garner the kind of broad-based appeal he will need. Anyone who has ever heard Lake argue a point, politely, but to the death, can attest that he will be able to provide a game plan.

But that is putting the independence cart before the horse, even while those around him clamor for him to lead.

Junior Lake, past, present and future all to be weighed, has a Shakespearian decision to make, a question to pose to himself and answer to his satisfaction only — "to be, or not to be."

August 1997

This is how things work here, or how they don't. We have a politician on St. Maarten named Elton Jones. In the last election he received less than 80 votes running with the Democratic Party. Now, he's an independent and has aligned himself with Julian Rollocks and the SAPP and by extension, the St. Maarten Patriotic Alliance. Reportedly, Elton has a problem controlling himself around women. Recently, Lydia Henderson, the pan-sexual freak who works at GBBC Radio, claimed Jones struck her and tried to choke her. This is serious enough, but the brilliant duo did not have their argument in some private boudoir. Nope, Elton allegedly smacked the girl down right in front of the government administration building, which is just a few steps from the police station. This happened in broad daylight. According to

Badejo, Elton has a history of this, having beaten another woman so badly she had to be hospitalized. This being St. Maarten, no one will verify it, but everyone will talk about it.

Lydia filed a police report, but then dropped charges, but not before dropping some bombs on Elton, saying the two of them had some real freaky shit between them, and that Elton was extra angry at her because he walked in on Lydia and Elton's common-law female something who were practicing vaginal CPR on each other or something like that.

Lydia says it's true, but no one really believes Lydia because she's as unstable as a three-legged table, and because she shot her credibility in the foot by dropping charges against lover boy Elton.

The bottom line is this, Jones is in line to be part of the Executive Council (EXCO) by virtue of his association with his new friends. EXCO, through a majority, controls the Island Council, which translates to much power and prestige, well as much as can be garnered here.

I wanted to do a piece on whether Jones was fit for office. Good luck. Neither the so-called feminists and "new breed" like Debbie Jack, nor respected women like Gracita

Arrindell or Claudette LaBega would say a word about it. The issue was never brought up in any forum and Elton was home free. One day, Elton is going to hurt someone again, maybe even kill them, and then, just maybe, someone will say something.

"I am moved by fancies that are curled
around these images and cling:
The notion of some infinitely gentle,
infinitely suffering thing."
TS Eliot

1998

Bad day in general. Bad year. The wife mess remains terrible and I remain in debauched exile on Lily Road, located in luxurious downtown Saunders.

Things have been tough enough, but the real shock today was hearing that Roy Cannegieter died. Actually, Roy had been dead for years, addled by drugs, mental illness and his own terrible history. It was an open sore of a secret that when Roy was a teen, sapped by his father's brutality against him and his mother, Roy snapped and killed his father with a machete. Cut his head clean off. By St. Maarten standards, he was a non-person after that, useful only for the luridness of his life as a topic of conversation and as an object of ridicule.

Roy was no Chris Rock, but he could be funny at times. You know, sort of Joe Pesci funny. As a rule, every Friday he asked me for at least three copies of the weekend Guardian. What would he want with three Guardians? Roy could read, but then again there's not that much to read in the Guardian. I knew he didn't sell them because face it, who would buy a Guardian from Roy? So why? "Over the weekend, its hard to find toilet paper," he said.

Another time he accosted me outside the Guardian and asked me for some money so he could dine at his favorite establishment, Kentucky Fried Chicken. It so happened I was down to my last few dollars and couldn't help him out. Anyway, Abigail Richardson walked by and Roy put the I'm hungry appeal on her, really laying it on thick. He told her his legs hurt and his hands were ruined from arthritis. She told him no and pushed him away. Then he dropped a tactical weapon on her. He knew she's part of a growing number of St. Maarteners who are born again Christians, and that she goes to church every Sunday night.

"I am a child of Christ too," Roy announced.

Abigail, who many allege is a thief, has other problems as well. If she is not the most fucked-up person on St. Maarten she's among the top three, a sociopath just waiting to happen. She's scarier than Roy because Roy is neither more nor less than what he is— nuts. Abigail can pass for sane in the way saccharine can pass for sugar, close, but ultimately cancerous. Roy is fucked in the head and doomed and he knows it. It's part of his charm. Compared to Abigail, he comes off like Fred Astaire, albeit a step or two slow, with more Thorazine about him than top hat and lace.

Pending mental patient Abigail dug into her purse and pulled out a bill. It was a $10, but she thought it was only a single and told Roy to take it and leave. She noticed her error and was about to retract the $10 bill just as the suddenly and newly graceful Roy deftly plucked it out of her hand. She screamed at him to give it back and started cursing. But Roy, that child of Christ, remarkably limber and $10 richer was long gone, wobbling down the street like a crack-head Charlie Chaplin, shoulders rolling and legs churning, making tracks for KFC.

It's ironic that he died in the hospital after living all those years on the street. I know that hospital is fucked up, but I never thought Roy would go there to die. Strange. He was not yet 43, three years older than me. He called me daddy, which if you knew Roy's history is definitely pause for thought.

Five years ago Roy said he would wash my car for $2. He made feeble attempts, his body twisted like a seahorse trying to give birth, quick to quit and promise to come back soon. Five years later, the car remained filthy and Roy's asking price went up to $10, though he was willing to negotiate. I don't know how much money I gave him over the years, it didn't matter. I can't imagine how much crack he's smoked and whatever else he's put in his body, which often reeked of urine and profound neglect.

In recent weeks, he became more and more erratic and aggressive despite his physical woes. I imagined his heart was pumping something like Drano and vinegar, or maybe that's my heart— all his blood bleached by chemicals, the sun and death presaged.

But that's all pointless conjecture now. This I do know— we're just two guys, one crazier than the other who managed to kill their fathers.

It's sunset now and in a few hours I'll see the moon over the pondfill, irrevocable proof that another day is gone and that Roy is gone to the dark from which he came.

Tonight I'll just fly away, see where my collection of pills takes me, how far I can go; far enough away from the sight of stillborn seahorses screaming for my help in a dark ocean.

Roy remix

Satan is a Soviet, that's what they told me in school. I lay on my back and watch the sky pink and blue like God puked up a load of baby clothes.

I've got bugs crawling inside my blood and my voice sounds like glass breaking. I run into the night hot and unhealthy. There is no place for me except this trapdoor in space and I've fallen through, and even though I was born, had a mother and am still breathing, I know I am already dead.

Spring, 1994

I'm sent to Anguilla to cover Queen Elizabeth's visit to that tiny island, nine miles from St. Martin. It's all bullshit, this pale faced inbred monarch checking out the progress of the happy darkies under her dominion. Hey Queenie, they don't look so happy. One kid sat on a wall as the Queen's entourage passed by and he sang, "I can see clearly now the Queen is here, I can see all obstacles in my way," not exactly what Johnny Nash had in mind, or for that matter Herald publisher and chief colonialist Roger Snow. Snowy-haired Roger's right in the middle of all this and I'm worried he might come all over the queen, as excited as he is.

The Guardian neglected to secure me a press pass which means I get to come as close to Elizabeth as the earth does to Jupiter. Just as well. I stay off in the shade and wait for the day to be over.

A guy in his late 30's walks by, blonde and tanned. Since I'm supposed to be getting some reaction to the queen's arrival, I ask the guy what he thinks.

"Honey," he says, "I'm from New York and I've already seen plenty of queens. What's one more?"

There's really only two questions I want to ask Queen Betsy: How does it feel to be an anachronism, is one, and what's your bra size is the other. Both will have to go unanswered.

September 1995

I guess I should write about Hurricane Luis, but I can't. I feel like everything is gone and now is the time to leave. I've got nothing new or original to say about the asshole hurricane which blew the roof off of our house in Colombier.

I've written about it in the Guardian and spoken to AP and read all kinds of local reportage on it and frankly, I've had it.

Almighty god is a living man, and woman, and child Reprinted from the St. Maarten Guardian, September 19, 1995

Enough personal, reportorial and photographic accounts about Hurricane Luis have already been promulgated to fill the Grand Canyon, with plenty left over to paper the walls of the Parliament Building on Backstreet. So, with that understood, why not one more.

Like so many others, my wife and I lost our roof and many of our possessions; they were, quite literally gone with the deafening wind into the Colombier night.

When my wife and I felt Luis de-roofing our house, we sat in the bathroom with our two dogs and waited for the eye of Luis to pass. We would have had more luck waiting for Godot, so we exercised plan B and chose to abandon ship and head next door to our neighbors who still had a roof.

A funny thing about walking into a hurricane, at least in retrospect. When you're indoors, it sounds noisily chaotic, like random gunfire. But when I stepped outside into the storm, either because I was so adrenalized or just plain numb, it felt as if it were absolutely still. I was aware of being drenched, but somehow I was walking through a vacuum, one hand holding my wife's shirt, the other holding the leash of a dog who probably thought this was an odd time to go for a walk.

When one steps into the maelstrom, one risks getting blown away; or getting smashed by debris, or simply disappearing into the night as if one never existed, passport and wallet in hand, a motherless child gone forever. Therefore, it is not unduly dramatic to say that when our neighbors opened their door, they saved our lives.

I am not one of those who subscribes to the notion that Luis was an act of God, either as punishment for sins committed, or as a second chance to do better. But neither do I rule out the spiritual aspects of the experience by any account.

In opening their door, and their hearts as neighbors, Yann and Nataly Darius and their three young children, angelically illustrated a belief voiced by one Robert Nesta Marley, "that almighty god is a living man," or in this case, man, woman and child.

Our neighbors took us in for nearly three weeks while our house was rebuilt. They fed us, lent us whatever we needed, and bolstered us against despair. They also dealt with more dogs and cats per square inch than Noah had to contend with on his Ark when he faced his own version of Waterworld and an angry Old Testament God who told him if he thought this was bad, "just wait till the fire next time."

My wife, who would have gotten along well with Noah, is a veterinarian. In preparation for the storm, she had taken in some 18 cats from the St. Martin Animal Shelter to join the five we already had at home for what she optimistically believed was safekeeping. The cats, like us, were transferred to the Darius home, and lived in a spare bathroom.

Add to this two large dogs, one not particularly smart and the other not particularly brave, and one can easily see why the Dariuses were one family who exceeded any and all bounds of human and animal kindness and patience.

A special word about Yann. If there is ever a nuclear war, I want to be on his side. He is absolutely amazing at handling any practical problem that might arise.

He's a professional diver who fixes boats, among other things. He and Nataly have known each other since they were children growing up in the Ivory Coast in Africa. He's a few years older than she is, so when they were young, he really didn't notice her as potential mate material.

"I thought she was just a baby," he said with a shrug.

Things obviously changed when they were teens, and now they have three children of their own, all of whom, by necessity, now like dogs.

Before Luis, we merely lived next door to each others. Now we are neighbors, and they are close to saints in my book. Merci Yann and Nataly, though it could never and will never be enough to thank you for everything.

It's obvious from looking around both sides of the island, that Luis has pushed many people toward their own particular moral, physical, financial and existential precipice, for better and for worse. The hurricane caused millions in damage and likely claimed at least two lives, though no official death toll has been announced.

Luis is now a bitter legend here, his nearly 180 mph gusts and rage fair enough credentials to make him the first Latino-named storm to be inducted into the hurricane hall of fame beside such killers as Hugo, David and Andrew.

Speaking of Andrew, I was in Florida earlier this year, and I drove through Homestead, ground zero for Andrew. The place had not so much been devastated as it was vaporized. Almost nothing was left standing. I asked a man who worked at the local radio station how things were going after the storm and he just looked past me like he was watching a funeral cortege. He and others had that thousand yard stare of people who had seen the unforgettable.

And so, here, what of Luis three weeks later? Is there meaning to Luis beyond cliche, homilies, bad poetry and the Weather Channel?

Is their luz, or light from Luis?

Shakespeare's King Lear raged against the mythic storm and lost, but ultimately won. He was stripped of delusion and ego; learned to love and found some sort of enlightenment.

Is this the meaning of Luis being shocked and devastated yet human enough to look into the proverbial heart of darkness to find moments of grace and truth among the ruins?

October, 1995

Went to New York to bury my grandfather. So much has happened in the past month. Hurricane Luis which decapitated our house, Hurricane Marilyn when it looked like it would never stop raining, and now grandpa.

It's as if the community of the dead keeps growing like a city inhabited by people you can no longer touch or see, but that you know are somewhere, only it's somewhere you can't get to.

I think of all the losses I've been through, father, grandparents, Louise, friends, pets, innocence... whatever, this is the loss that will stay with me, the loss that carries an adult weight and utter finality, because he was the only person I had made peace with and loved without ambivalence, and let go. He prepared me for it.

This is how life goes. When I was a boy, my grandfather would sometimes trim the hairs at the back of my neck with a safety razor and warm shaving cream. Years later, I put the warm soap on his face and shaved him, pressing the razor ever so lightly against his white beard growth. What I remember most is that he inched up a little and gave me a little nudge, the way a cat might when it felt warm and clean. I left him sleeping on that late summer afternoon, the sound of his breathing a shovel in damp earth.

This may seem a bit sentimental, maybe even trite, but I always felt that he refused to let me become a rogue comet hurtling through the sky, crash burning too early. He was the solid star, blank but fixed, that gave me the gravity to assume some kind of orbit. Electricity has finally been restored to Colombier after the hurricanes, but I turn all the lights off and sit on the porch and wait for it to get dark enough to search the sky, looking for errant comets and the old stars that watch them in the night.

Smack down
November-December1998

Don't really know how much more of this I can take. Smack down battle with wife at Guana Bay today with five Mormons taking photos to send back to Utah or wherever, looking on as my wife went Bruce Lee on me. Instead of a religious experience the children of the Church of Latter Day Saints, those milk-drinking, bicycle-riding, white shirt-wearing disciples of Brigham Young got their holy selves an eyeful. Enormous battle with wife over Dutch girl, my propensity for lying, my cowardice, the entire puke puke platter of disdain laid out by a wife for her husband.

My cheek still hurts from the frontal heel of the palm smack and my shoulder blade is killing me from her direct hits.

It's getting so that my own life is so hazardous, I'm in need of a stunt man. I did not hit her back. I didn't have the will. Or maybe

I was afraid that if I began hitting her I might not stop.

Anyway, my complete Kafkaesque diminishment, my transfiguration from human being into nothingness is almost finished. I'll be my own executioner. Just the way my dad taught me, just like I've always wanted. Yeah, that'll teach me. I can hear my own heart grinding down on itself, like some garbage disposal choking on a fork. It can't be over quickly enough. And now, another tonight, just like yesterday's tonight, living here on Lily Road, watching Party of Five where young Bailey's drinking is out of control, hey, join the club pal. I lay here, in the blue cast off TV light dry humping the sheets of soiled passion, all knotted up in a ball.

Wondering if I've turned some corner and fallen into a cistern in my head, some black hole where I'll come squirting out the other side like Lazarus.

I wonder if I now officially have a drug habit. My drug consumption is way out of control. I collect tranquilizers and sleeping pills from nice local doctors just like a mad little squirrel hoards more nuts than he will possibly need. I get kind attention from these doctors because I genuinely appear to look terrible and I always pay cash. These doctors who give me gentle warnings and sympathy and precious few lectures on drug dependency etc. before sending me on my not so merry way. It occurs to me I have more than enough in stock to kill myself, which crudely speaking, is the point of stockpiling.

In fact, I have more than enough here to start my own pharmacy, or better still, my very own Jonestown if I wanted, which I don't. I like my privacy and besides, I hate Koolaid. Anyway, I figure I'm in an altered state about 23 hours a day. It might sound trite, but it's the only way I can make it through all the guilt and shame about my life and wife, the boredom and bullshit at work and the emptiness and rage everywhere.

The whole Dutch girl thing will come crashing down on me soon, already has begun, as I've run out of emotional gasoline to keep anything going except my own special brand of controlled nuttiness. I know it's coming and I don't really know why I created the whole situation. Boredom, emptiness, loneliness. The diminishment of being married to someone increasingly critical and possessive? Who knows. Who cares? Technically, I should, but I don't, I don't feel much of anything, which means my drug and alcohol therapies are working, at least for now.

I can safely say I have become the asshole I always despised in others. My life has become some type of paper company/off-shore corporation empty shell, I've got no core, no address. I've become just like the people on this island that I'm always ragging on. There is no there there and no more me here. All that's left of me is my DNA— the sperm that drips out of me, some pubic hairs left in the bed and the droplets of blood that curl off my arm as I scar myself into recognition.

Excuse me church lady, but does that cross vibrate? July 1997

We live next door to a certified religious fanatic. She's a nurse from Guadeloupe who works night five times a week. In her spare time, she performs exorcisms and conducts liturgical services at night about 10 feet from our bedroom window.

If this were not enough, lately she's carrying on a wild affair with Mr. Jesus M. Christ himself.

One Saturday morning I'm laying in bed reading when I begin to hear all this heavy breathing and panting from next door.

Church lady, while a whack job, is attractive, and has no boyfriend I know of. So, I'm kind of curious about her passion.

This one Saturday morning church lady keeps saying, "oui petit Jesus, oui petit Jesus..." it keeps building, sort of her tantric sex with the savior, with her breathing getting more and more hot and heavy until after about 15 minutes of this, she screams out "oh, oh, oh, OUI Jesus, merci Jesus, oui, oui, mon petit Jesus."

Just your average French St. Martiner having an orgasm and a quiet morning at home with her boyfriend, the savior.

Once again I tell Jenny Li that I would prefer not to live next door to the immaculately deranged. She suggests ear plugs.

"You will respect my authority"
Eric Cartman, South Park, Colorado
October 1998

Me and Esther are listening to a particularly brutal and repetitive Island Council meeting on the radio. We have to, because as reporters it's our job, though we spend most of the time laughing and cursing at what the politrixters have to say. The chief buffoon is

William Marlin, leader of the St. Maarten Patriotic Alliance and the biggest asshole on St. Maarten, which believe me, is quite an achievement. He's the type of guy who likes to grab his crotch while he stares at the chest of female reporters. He is amazingly arrogant without having the slightest bit of cool, intelligence or character to back it up. He's bad, but he's far from alone. Sarah Wescott-Williams, leader of the Democratic Party has mastered the knack of speaking shrilly for 45 minutes without actually articulating a single original thought.

She's also become the queen of redundancy by constantly referring to "the youth as our future," as if the youth could be part of the past, and by saying things like "financial economic situations."

It's all just one long emotional harangue after another. They all take 30 self-aggrandizing, self-promoting minutes to say what could be said in three minutes. And every one of them has to refer to Lt. Gov. Dennis Richardson as "Mr. Chairman" at least 60,000 times. I kid you not. Listening to this shit for just a couple of hours causes worse brain damage than taking 10 hits of angel dust and topping it off with some industrial strength glue sniffing. It's like breathing pure polyester. It's like being in the middle of a big, incredibly fucked-up dysfunctional chicken-leg-eating incest ridden family where nothing is ever settled and passive aggressive oral masturbation passes for truth. I can almost see the spittle, all this verbal semen bouncing off of fiber glass walls.

Frankly, it's an assault on common sense, not to mention the senses in general.

Anyway, in the middle of this retarded form of democracy, I start to fantasize about going into the Albert Claude Wathey Legislative Hall armed with an AK-47 and opening fire on all of them. Watch them all go down. See their Rolex watches covered with blood; watch them all get cut to white ribbons, smoke rising and everything nice and quiet. Silence, finally, except for the ringing of their cell phones.

I'm thinking about taking round two into the streets when Esther comes over and switches off the radio. Says, "I can't take it any more."

Then looking at me with concern as I flex and unflex my trigger finger, she asks, "are you all right?'

Just fine little sister, just fine.

An Oxymoron Once And Always
Reprinted from the St. Maarten Guardian, March 24, 1998

The current coalition, the "government of empowerment" that comprises the lame duck Executive Council has now been in office more that six months. And, never has "empowerment" seemed so close to running on spiritual and political empty.

In fact, when dealing with that government's choice of a title, the operative phrase that applies is, once an oxymoron, always an oxymoron.

An oxymoron is a figure of speech with an apparent, inherent contradiction. For example: jumbo shrimp, military intelligence, honest politicians, and finally, "government of empowerment," though since its stinging political defeat in January, the term "government of empowerment" isn't used much anymore. Perhaps they've finally caught on.

How can you empower, or promise to empower, when you are essentially politically and financially powerless? How do you enable, ennoble and strengthen your people when you exist in what is basically a constitutional oxygen tent aerated by a colonial power? You don't. You are akin to a teenager living in your parents' home. You want to borrow the car, you have to ask permission. Need a few dollars? Go ask mom and dad. Your power is a nascent thing, not fully realized, and not likely to come of age until you do, and leave your parents' home.

This is not mere fancy. Developments in recent weeks on the insular government level, things that cannot be blamed on Curaçao or Holland, serve as semaphores that the government of empowerment has not delivered. Many, if not all major projects are at a halt, and the forces of entropy, not empowerment, are everywhere. There is absolutely no substantive, evidentiary sign of real progress. The harbor is on hold. Home porting for the Sunquest, which was to add $30 million to the local economy, is not going to happen this year.

The airport remains a chronic quagmire, stalled by lack of money, huge debts and misleading statements about outside investors. Add to this the Kadaster fiasco.

The island government, after long ignoring the land surveying office and saying no to a proposal from Holland to quasi-privatize it, is now going to have to figure out what to do with an understaffed department that has about $5 million in KABNA funding, yet is responsible for more than $5 billion worth of property registered to it.

There have been some accomplishments in six months, but exactly who beyond several commissioners, their executive assistants, and others who benefit from the perk-trickle down status quo has been empowered?

The problem is not a partisan one singular only to this bunch. In reality, it makes no difference who runs the Executive Council. Given the system and the way the insular government is positioned between the crenelated gears of The Hague and Willemstad, the result will be the same.

It's just that the government of empowerment set itself up by choosing such an august name with so little concept of what true empowerment is, and what kind of ideology and commitment is needed to back it up.

In the late 1980's and early 1990's empowerment was not a cliche, and meant something real in the United States; the growing hegemony in urban centers, grassroots activists spurred on by men like Jesse Jackson on a national level and growing numbers of African-American and Hispanic politicians on the local level, working to better things for disadvantaged people of color.

Much of the best of this work could be

seen in the large housing developments in cities like Boston and New York where community workers toiled ceaselessly, and at just better that minimum wage, to help eradicate the root causes of poverty, drug use and self abnegations. Much of this work was in concert with existing government, but not all of it.

In Boston, the radical minister Rev. Graylan Ellis-Hagler, working in the city's minority area, Roxbury, made it clear his job was to undermine the power structure, not to stroke it; to jolt it, like Jesus overturning the mercantile tables and driving the vendors out of the desecrated temple.

This government, while stridently Afro-Caribbean-St. Maarten-centric early on, and determined, is still dependent on Kingdom funding, and has been anything but visionary or radical. The colonial deck was stacked against them anyway.

As a genuine, but unlikely act of empowerment, something befitting a government in tune with its people and the future, the Executive Council should table a motion calling for another referendum; call in some fresh air.

Leave a legacy, do something far more meaningful than just a symbolic rehash of the

Concordia partition treaty. Do something that exists outside a colonial cliche.

After all, empowerment is only possible once you step out of the door in the house that confines you. Until you do, it's just something you talk about.

Auntie B—Raw!
Reprinted from the St. Maarten Guardian, May 22, 1998.

For nearly a decade Auntie B has responded to your letters about relationships, etiquette and child raising with polite professionalism.

But Auntie B gets other letters; crucial letters from a far more disturbed and politically challenged group of St. Martiners who test her acumen, and force her to utilize her degree in industrial psychiatric food and beverage management from the Louis Crastell Gumbs School of Applied Applications to come up with the right answers.

On Ascension Day, Auntie B shook out the very bottom of her crucial mailbag, and this is what descended. But first, a caveat. Auntie B had a discussion with Fernando Clark, the Ices: T and Cube, and the ghost

of Peter Tosh about the concept of "raw." Finally, Auntie B, actually Dr. Ing. Auntie B, M.A., (emotional) CPR, etc. etc... decided, after much emotional support from Clark to go "raw" for The Guardian in her answers to the following letters sent to her.
Here now, the letters:

Dear Auntie B, As an avid news watcher and reader, I've become aware that students and dissidents in Indonesia are dying for what they believe in. In Puerto Rico, they clamor for either independence or statehood, in Guadeloupe the students have rioted, and on the northern half of the island, anyone, anywhere will strike at the drop of a dime.
Here in St. Maarten, except for a peaceful night of "poetry" against the Franco-Dutch Treaty, we don't do much, unless it's some guys in big trucks driving in circles blocking things like they did five or so years ago. Why, with so much wrong, do St. Maarteners seem so complacent now? *Signed, the Revolution will not be televised.*

Dear Televised, This one has puzzled me for a while. You have a situation where the island's ecosystem is being destroyed, its constitutional future is stagnant, unemployment is rising, people are eating out of garbage cans, while others are lying and getting fat in the name of Jesus; its politicians lack heart and soul, and there are plans to build a hugely suspicious, hugely expensive waste disposal plant that some say will produce cancer causing gasses. And still, there is no real activism, no civil disobedience.

The problem is, that many of the island's so-called best and brightest, those who speak of liberation one day, work for the government and are loathe to give up security, a good paycheck, and bite the hand that feeds them for a "small thing" like a good cause, or the control of their own destiny.

The one thing that might get people into the streets is if their Cable TV or Fast Food rights (including Saturday barbecues) are taken away from them.

That could do it.

Dear Auntie B, I'm scheduled to have surgery at the St. Maarten Medical Center soon. It is supposedly not serious, but I will have to receive general anesthesia and I will be out for hours. I worry about not waking up. Is there any "natural" alternative to being put under with gas? *Signed, a scared young patient.*

Dear Scared Patient, My first response was no. But then earlier this week I was listening to the radio and I heard former errand boy, I mean, minister Danny Hassell, droning on and on forever in his mixture of accents talking about who knows what for 25 minutes. Frankly, I fell asleep, deep sleep, till 6 p.m. when I woke up and heard Nora Sneek-Gibbs doing the same thing upon which I fell asleep again. My suggestion, tape a solid three hours of various droners back to back. If you can stay awake, you might include Sen. Roland Tuitt, Will Johnson and any Curacao politician in the mix. Put on your headphones, relax, and believe me, you'll be out for hours.

Dear Auntie B, I notice that Sen. Roland Tuitt publishes and reads on the radio a lot of articles on economics, most notably Saranomics. Just what is he saying? What is Saranomics, and I don't recall exactly how the senator became a senator. *Signed, Confused.*

Dear Confused, Think of economics at least in St. Maarten, as a zero-sum game played not unlike dominoes under the very watchful eyes of the Florida Caribbean Cruise Association, American Airlines, BBW, and the

Kingdom Government. Tuitt would like to have you believe that Mrs. Wescott-Williams has no grasp of finances, but let's face it, dear, when studied closely, most St. Maarten economic theories, regardless of political affiliation, are about as sophisticated as a couple of 7-year olds setting up a lemonade stand.

As to how Mr. Tuitt became a senator, we refer you to the book of Vance, chapter one, verse seven; "and ye who are my friend, can hold my seat without stealing votes or thunder; nor venture into the kingdom of yon Duke William, and shall reign... for 9 months."

Dear Auntie B, Perhaps it is my own addled thinking, but are regular letter writers T. Eric Johnson, A.J. van Spanje, James E. Maduro, and Deja Vu the same person? *Signed, Hard to tell them apart.*

Dear Hard, you might have something there. They have never been seen together in the same room. It's a theory worth checking out.

Even dwarfs start small
October, 1998

Went to the dentist for a tooth that seemed to be imploding into my head and he performed the dreaded root canal which entails reaming out the offending molar with what seemed like a crow bar. The one good thing is that I now have in my possession a nice little pain killer called Percocet, and tell me, who's more deserving of being relieved of his pain than I am? I took a couple of them last night and sat down with a yellow legal pad next to me, staring, and not much happened, at least I thought, until three hours passed and I realized I hadn't moved at all, the yellow pad still at my side, and I forgot I ever had any teeth, let alone a screaming molar.

Anyway, I went back for seconds, and then I passed out again and dreamt of dwarfs dancing around a tree, and stuffed animals in an FAO Schwarz toy store singing and dancing along to the theme from New York, New York, expertly lip synching to Frank Sinatra.

When I woke up, I remembered that a few days ago I'd seen the only dwarf I'd ever encountered on St. Maarten. I was driving by with Pamela Sims, a woman from the humane society who goes around giving some St. Maarten dogs tick and flea baths and gathering up other unlucky mutts for the gas chambers at the vet clinic run by the phony white angels of death, when I saw him. He was maybe seven, with the telltale stubby legs and big head. He lived in a section called the Garden of Eden, which is anything but. He was playing with a few other children, and for now, they were the same height.

He looked like he could use a bath, but Pamela wasn't looking at him. I guess things will change soon, and the boy will begin to see everyone get bigger like they're passing him on a genetic escalator. The last thing I can recall was that the boy was rubbing his hand over his head, as if summoning a genie out of the hot air for wishes sake.

Child Abuse: What Would You Do?
Reprinted from the St. Maarten Guardian, October 7, 1998

There is a six-year-old girl in La Savane whose back looks like a road map of rage. There is not an inch of her small slender back that is not flayed, that has not been covered by the heavy slap of a leather belt against a child's soft skin.

Look, and there are belt marks on top of marks, the wounds piled over one another. Look closer, and you can see the imprint of a belt buckle on her back and shoulder, another on her left arm.

Does the pain ever stop for this little girl, and why is she being so abused? What's her crime, having been born?

There is a caring and brave neighbor who hears the cries. She knows the girl is being beaten by her father, who may or may not be her biological father. He is unemployed. His wife works all day. He wears clothing that advertises brand names, like Nike. He apparently swings a belt like Tiger Woods swings a golf club.

Last week, the neighbor's 12-year-old, who is fond of the girl and her siblings who live perhaps 30 feet away from her, brought the girl over to her home. She asked the six-year-old to show her mother what she had already seen.

The quiet little girl was hesitant, but eventually she raised her T-shirt and showed two adults and a 12-year-old her war zone of a back.

The neighbor, her husband and her 12-year-old daughter are European. The abused girl, her mother and father and three younger siblings are from another island in the Caribbean.

When you know a child is being beaten, what do you do? It's a complicated matter anywhere. For one, most people are hesitant about getting involved, either because they don't think it's their business to interfere with how another family chooses to rear its children, or because they think they might make matters worse, either in the form of reprisals against the child in question, or the person or persons intervening.

Also, if you are a white European living in the Caribbean, there is a built-in awkwardness, a sense of cultural clumsiness. What are the boundaries? Does one think I am not allowed to say something even though something terrible is going on because I am not from here?

Obviously, child abuse cuts across all lines, all races, all ethnicities and all classes. The purpose of this is not to single out one type of people as opposed to another. The one constant in all abuse cases, is that the child is never to blame. There is no earthly reason, no justification for anyone to beat away a child's innocence and trust and replace it with cruelly-raised flesh covering scars that cover psychic wounds that may never heal. It's soul murder.

For this neighbor, there was no question. Something had to be done.

"I had to. This was not right and I did not want my 12-year-old daughter thinking this is the way things should be done."

The neighbor spoke with the girl's mother. It seems the girl was beaten most recently because she went off with a friend to have her hair plaited and left her two-year old sibling unattended.

"She a bad one," the mother said in Creole, dismissing the point that a six-year-old should not be left in charge of a two-year old, especially if there is an unemployed father who can do the baby-sitting in the first place. Last Thursday, my wife alerted the police about the little girl and a policeman arrived along with an educator who specializes in social service issues.

They did not find the father, but they found the girl and both officials determined the girl was being beaten beyond any definition of normal discipline.

The husband of the woman who wished to help the girl panicked when he saw the officials. He said he did not want them involved. He said if he saw the father raise a hand to the little girl again, he would beat the man up himself. Violence begetting violence, begetting more violence.

The official said the child would be monitored in school by teachers. Maybe you suspect a child is being abused. What would you do? Would you risk intervening and suffering the possible reprisals that might occur in a small society, especially where there are no real facilities in place to deal adequately with the issue?

Or would you do what you could to salvage a piece of childhood innocence from being beaten away forever, step in and be courageous and maybe save a life in the process, because some abuse cases do end in death, and every six-year-old has the right to turn seven.

To me, there is only one choice.

July 1998

Ran into Ras Lion today. He was sitting on Frontstreet cursing the tourists. He greeted me the way he always does. "I hate fucking white people." Well, me too. I hate everybody. So I don't take it personally. Besides, after a while, Lion refines his mad rant to the point where the only people he really hates, really wants dead, is "the Curaçao man," who he claims has robbed him of his chance to play soccer for the national team and who ripped off his music and purportedly made millions off it in Holland.

I don't know the particulars of all this, but I've heard it enough times so that I can catch the nuances when they occur. Such as his ever-changing number of children and grandchildren. Sometimes it's 4 and 8, other times 6 and 12. It's never an odd number. Later, I see him walking on the side of the road and offer him a ride. He climbs in with the usual greeting about white people. And I say, "yes I know. And when the revolution comes I'll be the first to go."

He nods at that, shows me some missing teeth, but says nothing. I drop him off at his small house in Agrement. Before I leave he tells me to wait and roots around for a few moments before handing me some callaloo, a small pumpkin and some peppers. I'm still not convinced that I won't be the first to go.

August 1995
Ronny Redux

I finally found out what happened to Ronny Peterson. It seems he got busted smuggling Chinese nationals into U.S. territory en route from St. Maarten. Ronny denied he was smuggling and said he was performing a humanitarian act in bringing the Chinese into political asylum. He spent a total of six months in jail after copping a plea to avoid a long jail sentence. Strange how he walked into the Guardian with all his court papers and his arguments. I like the guy, but the fact is he did get paid to transport human beings illegally from one point to another. Now he's talking about how hard it is for him to get a job and how in spite of the fact he was a guest of the U.S. government in their Puerto Rican hellhole, he just might consider doing it again. Bad move Ronny. Better stay on dry land and away from the Chinese smuggling mafia at the Pitusa Hotel.

Five years old
February 1994

The Guardian turned five today. Five years of trying to fight the good fight. I've only been here a few months, but man, what a weird crew.

Dutch Debbie and Lady Sha sell ads. I think they sell other things, not drugs, but you know, services in exchange for cash. Trevor Thorpe does sports and entertainment and seems like a creature forever frozen in the 1970's. I've noticed that in addition to fancying himself a ladies' man, he's unbelievably homophobic and full of shit.

He goes on and on about "bullahs," Bajan (Barbadian) for gays. It's like he doth protest too much. Strange, how he shuts up when Bevil comes in the Guardian offices. Bevil is a former Guardian employee and one of the few openly gay men on St. Maarten. I think Trevor knows that if he said something insulting about gays in Bevil's presence, Bevil would kick his ignorant ass back to Barbados.

Like Joe Dominique says about Trevor: "knows everything, knows nothing."

We were listening to the radio the other day when "I Shot the Sheriff" came on, the Eric Clapton version. Nothing bad about that except Barbados-born, African-Caribbean hot shot Trevor thought it was Clapton who wrote the song, not some genius immortal named Robert Nesta Marley.

Editor Fabian is a nice guy, but I can tell there's too much on his plate and he lacks focus. He's at the Guardian six days a week, at least 12 hours a day trying to keep tabs on everything from advertising to political gossip to news editing. He's an excellent editorial writer and political reporter. It's unfortunate he's spread so thin, or more accurately, that he's chosen to spread himself so thin.

After working on newspapers stateside, I can see right away things are done a lot differently here, not just at the Guardian, but at the rival Herald and Chronicle as well, and what passes for news and "ethical journalism" would never make it in the states.

Still it's a challenge of sorts, and maybe I'll break some new ground. So far, everyone has been pretty nice to me.

I'd be remiss if I didn't say something about Abigail. More than anyone, she basically gets paid for doing absolutely nothing. She's supposed to be a photographer, but as far as I can tell, all she does all day is eat, listen to the radio and go shopping on Backstreet.

On several odious occasions, I had to drive her to an assignment where she would photograph the back of some's head. Talk about driving Miss Lazy, or Miss Crazy.

I've seen her go off on Badejo verbally, and that coupled with her uselessness, makes me wonder how she's stays employed. Wait, I know the answer to that, but I guess it's just rumor mongering.

Speaking of being sticky, recently, Dutch Debbie has complained that money has gone missing from her purse. Others have said the same thing. In a rare lucid moment, Dutch Debbie said she was sure Abigail was the culprit and if it happens a next time, she'd call the police.

Meanwhile, Lady Sha is screaming, literally, that Dutch Debbie is "poaching" her clients and thus stealing her advertising commissions. Dutch Debbie better be careful because I don't doubt for an instant that Lady Sha is an assault case ready to happen, especially when the subject is money, hers.

Shackles raising hackles

One cannot live in the Caribbean for any length of time and not be confronted by the white guilt issue, the cosmic question: Must I individually, solely by virtue of race, share responsibility for the systematic horrors of slavery. Am I automatically linked to a heinous past because I am white?

The whole concept of slavery, the African Diaspora, whether it's the Caribbean or United States, is difficult to grasp. Imagine the worst, and then go from there.

On St. Maarten, the legacy of slavery cuts deep and wide. You can see the vestiges of it in the plantation style politics, unresolved social issues, racism, and ruinous, petty self-hatred.

You can also see how it's been perpetuated in the sense that the island is almost wholly dependent on large ships that bring cash cows called tourists, not slaves, and lock the economy of St. Maarten into a perceived subservience and dependency on North American money. This familiarity breeds contempt.

I've noticed a lot of St. Maarteners have taken it upon themselves to learn more about African history and their lineage. This is commendable, of course. But here's the St. Maarten virus at work.

There's this young guy named Hondo Rami and he's a devotee of all things black and African. Badejo regularly prints things he writes, pertaining to celebrations like Kwanza and other pieces dealing with slavery. One day, Badejo calls me into his office and tells me to take a look at his computer screen. Up there is Hondo's latest piece, the usual, but about three paragraphs down there's a note in the text to see photo 12a on page 73. Well, well. Hondo's been copying the stuff out of a book and taking credit for it.

Badejo says he's going to call Hondo on it, and set a trap for him, next time. Badejo lets the story run and takes out the reference to the photo. Fabian is inexplicable at times. His soft heart and generosity of spirit often works in my favor, so there's no sense me calling him on it.

For however many St. Maarteners who actively explore their African connections, I've also come across those who refer to my boss Fabian Badejo, a Nigerian, and radio man Eddie Williams of Sierra Leone, as "you Africans." It's not said warmly. Abigail and other former Guardian employees call Badejo's kids "the Africans."

Why the edge? I'm not sure. I think Africa looms as the great mother breast for so many who feel the need for a nurturence unpolluted by forced exile and no weaning. A promised land, much the same way Israel is for Jews.

But what do you make of St. Maarteners who seemingly trivialize slavery by constantly referring back to images of shackles and middle passages in trite poems, but without any nuance or feeling. No passion, no ambivalence, no exploration of how this legacy has led to a culture of poverty full of quick fix money-related fixations, no creative redirection of their lifeline to the past.

For instance, nobody explores the topic of what they might actually do, how they would fit in or not fit, if they did go to Africa and seek a new life.

Despite their intentions, they make slavery and Africa a cliche, a comfortable niche, a stereotype rather than an archetype. Sekou wrote a very good story about a slave's passage in his quartet of short stories called The Brotherhood of the Spurs. But much else on St. Maarten relevant to the subject falls short of casting a new light, or new paths to be taken based on a knowledge of one's past, or shucking off what scholars refer to as nostalgic masochism.

I suppose its the ontogeny and phylogeny of any organism trying to give birth to a new self: it's bound to recapitulate the past until the point it's safe to be reborn.

But what about the notion of shared responsibility?

Can I, as a Jew, rationally blame Germans born 50 years after Hitler for being part of the Holocaust? I don't know. Maybe this factor, the inbred smell of incinerated Jewish flesh in my cerebral cortex, gives me a little window to peer out of and if need be, escape from on the slavery issue because I've had family members exterminated in the name of madness, and others cast into the wind penniless and broken, children of another Diaspora.

My wife says she understands how slavery has left the Caribbean with such a treacherous legacy, and is more empathic. For me, it's more a case of being in tune with the collective unconscious of all those who have been oppressed, a matter of sensitivity to suffering.

It's a tough trick courting the past and then trying to step into the future, something always calls you back to your atavistic past.

I guess that's my post-modernist answer: no matter what your past is, it's one thing knowing your history and another being trapped by it.

I've never felt responsible for enslaving anyone, except of course, myself.

An enduring Taboo
Reprinted from the St. Maarten Guardian
September 28, 1998

Race. It is our most enduring taboo, the bugaboo that hangs on to our atavistic selves, causing us to become a humpbacked species. Think about what is going on with Commissioner Julian Rollocks and his fascination with African-American tourists and the reactions to it.

The commissioner said in an interview with an American publication that he wanted to replace 100,000 of St. Maarten's current tourists with 100,000 African American tourists.

Is his goal needlessly separatist and divisive, not to mention ill-advised, or is it one man's attempt to express the totality of his Blackness at age 42?

Has Rollocks embraced W.E.B. Du Bois' credo, "that I shall be as Black as blackness can, the darker the mantle, the mightier the man," or is his courting of one tourism group at the sake of another a form of racial fascism? Or, are those opposed to it racist in their way?

Think about that "Poem For Maria" and the words that are taken for granted here and used on the floor of the Island Council. Words like mulatto, mulatta and mestiza, words that hearken back to the racial fractionalization of slavery and the internalized self-hatred and inbred definitions it spawned. The issue is not Rollocks, the issue is race.

Are you a racist? And how would you define it? Is it an artificial, social construct or something that is part of our species? Do you judge me, look at me on the basis of skin color? Do I do the same to you? Can I not identify with you because you do not mirror me racially?

Do you blame me for slavery? Do I overcompensate and think myself inferior to you because I could never explain, nor exculpate myself from my historical connection to oppression and genocide?

Is my genetic material stained by the blood of the oppressor? Is yours ennobled by being oppressed?

Is my white skin a tattoo; a marking? Am I, or are you Ishmael? Is white skin the perfect passport in a world where Caucasians have long called the shots, or is it somehow a liability as global geopolitics change and the earth becomes increasingly populated by people of color.

Are we all not prisoners in the castles of our own skin? Surrounded by moats in which swim ancient alligators who have swallowed all of us regardless of melanin content?

It is absolutely time we speak about race here on St. Maarten. It is not an issue to be debated on the floor of the Island Council, or literally fought about in French Quarter or Marigot, but one to be discussed thoughtfully, provocatively and openly in a forum at a venue like Axum.

My boss and friend Fabian Badejo, who is perhaps as open minded on the subject of race as anyone I have ever met, has suggested the way people in St. Maarten describe others in gradations ranging from "blue black" to "red" to "clear" to dark to white to whatever; the open use of the words mulatto and mulatta, which in the United States are considered terms almost as offensive as nigger, makes St. Maarten in some odd ways more like the South Africa of the Apartheid era than one would like to think.

In the United States the buzzwords for the

past decade have been empowerment, multiculturalism and diversity. Americans have been race crazy for years. Historically, in the United States, if you had one drop of "Black blood" in you, you were considered a "person of color".

Multiculturalism is a recent phenomenon that helped to address the temporal matter of inclusion, if not the existential issue of race.

Those inclusive concepts that Americans have tried to artificially graft onto society have been innate to this region adding much to its richness and allure.

The subject of race on St. Maarten, as Badejo pointed out, has been a subtle one for a long time. It is no longer so subtle.
I share Rollocks' fascination with African-Americans.

The writer Albert Murray pointed out a long time ago that the dominant cultural idiom in the United States, even as manifested in slang, has always been African-American.

From jazz and blues to basketball and bebop, rhythm and blues to hip hop and rap — look at all those white boys walking around looking like they're gang bangers and talking like they just stepped out of the hood in South Central, the racial majority has always taken its hipness clues from a population it has tried to marginalize. Is that racist?

When I was a reporter in South Carolina in 1992, an old man told me the soil was so red, red like clay, because of all the blood that had seeped into the earth from lynched and mutilated Black men. I remember his face was expressionless as he stared into southern nothingness, but his hands were trembling.

Nothing would grow in that soil.

The experience spoke of the chasm of race, of what the late writer James Baldwin in *The Evidence of Things Not Seen* referred to as the cosmically painful experience of trying to "imitate a people (whites) whose existence appears, mainly, to be tolerable by their bottomless gratitude that they are not, thank heaven, you."

Talk away the taboo of race. Get real and honest about it, stop feeding those alligators. Now is as good a time as any to set up something meaningful at Axum and describe the evidence of things unseen; confront the chasm.

I must be guilty of something...
December 1998

I've been living out of the house in Colombier for a month . Residing on Lily Road, my forays into deviance an established routine now. Met my wife Jenny Li today at Anand's, a local Indian restaurant, and she looked really nice and composed like she was doing much better. She was wearing this yellow dress that made her look like Audrey Hepburn and I was hoping things would stay civil and calm because I can't take any more dramatics, and I don't need any public explosions, especially since Wim, Dutch Girl's colleague from the Herald is sitting a few booths away, nursing what appears to be his third beer.

After what passes for several moments as a truce, inevitably the subject comes up and for me it's a steady 30 minutes of fending off countless questions I cannot hope to answer, the words and emotions no longer exist in my lexicon for living.

Though this has quickly turned to shit, and the Indian waiters among us are giving us a wide berth, taking away the uneaten palak paneer and raita before they can be used as weapons, I cannot help admiring her. She's relentless, like a Newtonian law of physics in a pretty little yellow dress, atoms trembling in her wake.

Later, after some pharmaceutical repair, I finally realize what is happening. By focusing all of her abandonment fears and hopes for love squarely upon flawed and fucked-up me, she has given me the ostensible, crushing power, the sole discretion to ruin her life.

And, because of my inability to do so, my inability to be able to even live my own life, let alone ruin her's, she has rendered me utterly impotent.

Why not a mud-wrestling Contest to Raise Funds for St. Martin's Entry to the Miss World Pageant? Reprinted from the St. Maarten Guardian, October 27, 1998

It's time for Myrtille Brookson to start helping herself. Segments of the St. Maarten population have already done their part rallying behind her $60,000 effort to get to the Seychelles to compete in the Miss World contest by staging a gala benefit dinner and fashion show, and most recently, a misogynist cross dressing extravaganza Saturday that netted Brookson another $2,500 bringing her grand total in funds raised for a specious cause to $40,000.

Reportedly, even the island government, which was last seen on bent knees before The Hague reciting the mantra, "win, win, win," interspersed with "please, please, please," in best James Brown fashion, the same island government which in more than three years has not seen fit to help the poor and deteriorating Roy Cannegieter replace his roof, kicked in some funds to send Myrtille on her way.

But Myrtille, despite her stature, still finds herself short. Of funds. This is troubling to me, because in my latest incarnation as a shallow booster of beauty and a lover of things that will put St. Maarten on the map and bring ever increasing cigar-smoking, gambling T-shirt buyers, er, I mean niche market tourists to the island, I am deeply troubled. So, I've come up with a way to help Myrtille help herself.

But I need the help of Christine Williams, former model and beauty queen, and current telephone company spokesperson and bodybuilder. Recently, Myrtille and Christine were photographed together as Tel-em did its part to keep Myrtille in contact with a cellular phone.

But that photograph of two beauty queens, one in her early 20's, the other . . . er older, set something off in my gauche, primal male mind. Here's how it goes. St. Maarten is a very messed up place. We put undue emphasis on beauty, money, radio shows, and partisan politics that go nowhere. We give little consideration to the poor, independence, spontaneity of thought and nonconformist imagination. Too many of us, male and female alike, are caught in the lace bars of the beauty jail cell.

With all that as a given, here's the way Myrtille's going to make up what she needs to get to the Seychelles in style. I propose a mud wrestling match between Myrtille and Christine Williams to be held at a venue to be chosen soon. Perhaps the offices of Laser 101, the Seaman's Club, or maybe in front of the White Virgin statues by the Catholic Church (hint, hint) or maybe at Hooters, which is what this is about anyway.

Ticket prices are as follows, $50 for men; women free if accompanied by a man. If a man wants to get splashed by mud, he has to pay an additional $50. If a man, or if any woman wants to get in the ring, the price is $200. If Glen Carty wants to make it a threesome, it's $500.

All donations are tax deductible and everybody gets a small package of Manal laundry detergent and a DP T-shirt (or a "Movin' on" sticker) as a parting gift.

Radio and TV "personality" Elton Richardson, who was part of the cross-dressing benefit for Myrtille Saturday, and showed he knew how to get in touch with his female side, perhaps a little too well (memo to Elton, stroking your "breast" like that Saturday night was a bit too convincing) will referee. After the mud, we'll move on to Jello wrestling. My prediction is Christine will win; she is stronger, more experienced and quicker, due to all that weight training. All proceeds will go to sending Myrtille to the Seychelles for that ultra-important event of being one of 100-plus women to be wasting their time and dignity in an anachronistic display of phoniness.

But my prejudice is getting ahead of my prose, so let me slow down. Before the threats of deportation start, let me make it clear that both Myrtille and Christine are nice women and the point is not to make them objects of ridicule simply because they are attractive and have likely gotten a lot of mileage out of their winning and winsome genetics.

But don't you find there's a bit of a problem with the community mobilizing so quickly to raise $60,00 for a beauty pageant when many St. Maartener's are truly destitute and desperate? All those armed robberies and break-ins are no coincidence.

Bad luck Roy Cannegieter and his woeful roof is just one example. What about people who are eating out of garbage dumpsters? What about the lack of teachers? It seems that $60,000 could pay three teachers' salaries couldn't it? The same amount of money could also be used to renovate the Upper Princess Quarter Hotel and turn it into a half-way house for recovering drug addicts. Wouldn't $60,000 go a long way to making a new cultural center a reality, or funding a political campaign for the St. Maarten Independence Foundation, or making the Senior Citizens' Recreational Center come to life?

Wouldn't $60,000 take care of a lot of medical needs?

Speaking of $60,000, isn't Myrtille a law student, and aren't many other young St. Maarteners scrambling around for funds for college? Kenneth Cook had to literally sweat, pray and cook chicken legs to raise enough money to get to the University of the Virgin Islands in St. Thomas. Zahira Hilliman's scholarship request got caught in red tape and politics. Maybe she should enter a beauty contest next time around. It's the fly girls who seem to draw the honey, I mean money. But let's not worry about that or anything else of consequence. There's mud wrestling and other beauty fund-raisers in the future. Remember, we can always raise money with a mixed gender wet T-shirt contest. Right Laser 101? Right Elton? Right?

January 1998

A lot of what goes on here is fueled by religion. Such a paradoxical island, yet such a symmetrical island. All in all, it really is Sodom and Gomorrah, with its casinos, hustlers, churches and saviors. People cannot sin fast enough in order to fill all the churches they've erected here in the name of redemption. Some of the churches are palatial, such as the Seventh Day Adventist Church. Other churches are no more than storefronts with several congregants and a sweaty preacher yelling in the night.

If there is any competition between Mosera and me it is who gets to be Jesus Christ when it's time to tear this place down and watch it all turn to salt. Who gets to overturn the tables in the casinos, who gets to chase out the hypocrites, who gets... well, who gets to wash the feet of prostitutes. Now this Christ thing is serious, not blasphemous. I think we both see Christ more as a creative genius than as a religious savior.

"He wasn't a pacifist, he was a rough guy. He had to deal with the fishermen and they were tough," Mosera tells me, adding the Book of Isaiah makes it clear Jesus was a rude boy, not a sanctimonious stuffed shirt preaching for money and dealing for the honeys.

I agree. Jesus, the political, historical character is a hero of mine. He was the supreme individualist, a rebel with a cause who accepted imperfection and embraced the ignorant and downtrodden. He was breathtakingly original. In the truest sense of performance art, he invented himself in a dangerous time and place.

I'm sick of Jesus being abused here by every hypocrite and crackpot using his name to explain and /or justify everything under the sun. Jesus was baffingly original, he issued challenges to conformity, he dared to be ecstatic. The application of Christianity here on St. Maarten is just the opposite. It makes everything so certain, so safe, so preordained.

People drive around in cars that carry bumper stickers that read, "Christians are not perfect, just saved."

And, it's used to make money, all over the world and here too. You ever stop to think how much money is collected in the name of Jesus? Check out those freak show religious programs on St. Maarten Cable TV, the ones with Benny Hinn and his puffed hair and that blond woman with her purple fright wig, testifying and collecting money in the name of miracles. Only miracle I'd like to see is to have one of those charlatans admit on TV in front of all the cripples, starving Africans and white trash basket cases they purport to be praying for, that the whole thing is a con game, a hustle. Would God, in his or her everlasting wisdom and innate sense of style and cool, even think twice about taking Benny Hinn seriously?

Also, think about how many people have been killed in the name of Jesus and Christianity, a religion that evolved in the centuries following his death and has grown steadily more at odds with his teachings and beliefs as the years go by and the dollars of the desperate flow in.

Jesus treated worldly goods as something to be despised, the complete antithesis of brand name St. Maarten with its Rolex watches, big cigars, sport utility vehicles and gold.

One day, Mosera and I muse about Jesus walking down Frontstreet in his robes and sandals. Only no one recognizes him, though they all wear t-shirts that say "I love Jesus," and "Big up Jesus."

Jesus walks up and down Frontstreet looking for true believers and warriors to help him finish his redemptive work, but he cannot find any. He eventually gets frustrated after too many people hand him flyers for timeshares complete with $75 rebates, or offer him $1 beers and then suck their teeth when he declines. There are so many kinds of prostitutes, he can't focus on just one to protect.

Jesus reads the writing on the wall and realizes this place cannot be saved, even by him, and like most sensible and discerning people heads to Marigot for dinner with the fishermen, and then a quick trip to St. Barts. A reporter from the Daily Herald (certainly a God-fearing newspaper if there ever was one, complete with a shady minister) catches up with Jesus and asks him if he would like to appear at a benefit to raise $70,000 so some young woman can attend the Miss World beauty pageant and come in 106th out of 107 contestants, the 107th being a test model female robot designed especially for pageants, but not yet bathing suit friendly.

The next day's imaginary yet utterly possible Herald story on Jesus reads like this: "The man, J.C., surrounded by 12 fishermen, was spotted by the Herald having dinner in Marigot. According to restaurant manager P.P., the man, J.C. amused his friends by turning water into wine.

P.P was furious about this, as it was cutting into profits. The Gendarmes were called and the man J.C. was given a stern warning. He and his friends are awaiting deportation to Galilee.

Said the man J.C. following his arrest, "the doors of the soul of this community are unhinged."

Oscar Wilde said it best about Jesus: "Christ, like all fascinating personalities had the power of not merely saying beautiful things himself, but of making other people say beautiful things to him." If only it were so in St. Maarten.

Ghost

In his dreams he is free; a creature of both air and water. In waking life, there are a thousand truths he cannot admit. In waking life, if you try hard enough, you can forget almost everything- your name, the smell of rain, what a tear tastes like.

Try hard enough, and you can forget you were ever born.

But awake or dreaming, there is one thing he cannot forget. It is her. He cannot say why she inhabits him so. It is not the promise of breasts or the taste of lips; it is everything. When his heart beats, it breaks. In his dreams, she breaks the surface of the water and he follows her down, though she cannot see him. He watches her swim beside grinning dolphins, their gray heads gleaming, nudging him ever closer to something he cannot describe.

Media Ownership on SXM & The Practice of Journalism Reprinted from St. Maarten Guardian, July 10, 1998

Reports have it that Rupert Murdoch backed off on a plan Wednesday to buy every media house in St. Maarten. It didn't happen. He turned his kangaroo around, refueled his private jet, and headed back to Los Angeles, deprived of some prime St. Maarten media.

Maybe he changed his mind because he was afraid of Commissioner Julian Rollocks. Or maybe, he didn't want to infringe on the turf of Ambassador Hushang Ansari. Rollocks Wednesday, on PJD-2 Radio, blasted the fact that his nemesis, Ansari, of the long dormant Mullet Bay Hotel, had bought GBBC Radio and apparently had closed a deal to purchase The Chronicle, one of St. Maarten's three daily newspapers.

Rollocks said he would look into the possibility of legislation to prevent the monopolization of media houses by a single ownership entity.

"Imagine people having this amount of money... if one man, one group, owns all the media on St. Maarten, it's going to be a very sad day," Rollocks said.

Let's forget about "sad" days for a moment, and take a reality check here.

For one thing, the commissioner, like all of his peers and would-be successors, needs to be in the spotlight. And what other spotlight is there but the media house, or houses, of your choice?

A prime example occurred Thursday when Rollocks, alarmed by a hand grenade the St. Maarten Hospitality and Trade Association tossed his way concerning his performance as tourism commissioner, summarily summoned all the members of the media he could contact, many of whom he no longer returns phone calls to, in order to give his spin and his position. Many came running; media manipulation as usual. He came armed with statistics to prove his various points, statistics that would not normally be assembled or made available unless a commissioner has a point to prove.

Rollocks is certainly not alone in this regard. Last week William Marlin, stung about reports concerning the Tower Air non-deal, decided at the 11th hour to open up his files on the matter. To everyone. Like Rollocks, the chances of his making those files public prior to a printed challenge would be as unlikely as an igloo in Aruba.

Of all the commissioners, none has been better traditionally at using the various media over a long term basis — from inchoate politician to established commissioner - than Rollocks. He's always had a feel for it, and has felt a freedom in going to the well many times, beginning with his lean "bread and butter" SAPP days when he delivered his hand written press releases on yellow legal pad pages and spent hours talking freely about his plans and hopes.

Rollocks spoke Wednesday about his fear that the media might be controlled. Seemingly noble, but also disingenuous. It was Rollocks who once admitted he snubbed the former GIS meet-the-press format on Wednesday mornings because he did not want to be surprised by any unplanned, live media questions and did not want to give up that control.

What's his fear now? If Ansari buys the whole pot, which he will not, is Rollocks most concerned about just how he and other politicians will get their selective messages out in the future?

Let's get back to that sad day when the "free" media of St. Maarten might no longer exist. It could be argued that the state of print and radio journalism is in may ways already a sad affair in St. Maarten.

In an indirect way, Rollocks might have opened up a Pandora's Box of sorts as it pertains to the quality and depth of journalism in St. Maarten, and where it might be heading. Remember, a seemingly "free" and virtually uncensored press is not the same as a strong, independent press.

Journalists are already far too collegial with politicians and other public figures; too much air and print time is devoted to self-serving tit-for-tats and one upmanship. Fawning attention is paid to dissembling public figures who exhibit no ideological distinction and who are defined wholly by partisan affiliation and cults of popularity, leading in some cases to a rah, rah banality of reportage that is very rarely memorable or meaningful given the inherent limitations of the practice on the island.

With a lack of public records, no real access to government papers and documents, no workable, credible, and practical local equivalent to the American Freedom of Information Act thus truncating the possibility of real, investigative journalism that might lead to something substantive, the language of journalism rather than thriving in this "free" environment, is being held hostage to crumbs thrown to reporters from politicians.

That hostage-held language becomes even more strangulated if a media house becomes ostracized by the commissioners because it does not readily assume the cheerleading or non-questioning mode expected.

A media house would then look for "real" news from other sources because no documentation or comments would be forthcoming locally, thus leading to charges from commissioners that such reports are "malicious" and "negative."

Because commissioners do not utilize press secretaries or empower aides to speak on their behalf, because GIS functions as a quasi-clearing house/public relations firm for the government, real, useful information remains scarce, and the notion of a free press remains an oxymoron.

In the unlikely event of monopolistic ownership changes, the onus would have to be upon journalists, in fact it is upon us now, to call for meaningful changes in terms of access to information and public records. Then we can be "empowered" to practice our profession as we should and establish some objective distance from the daily political push and pull, which more and more seems to resemble the cartoon shenanigans of the "Tom and Jerry Show."

Ultimately, in terms of what passes for news in St. Maarten, does it matter who buys what? Even if Ansari, Murdoch and Tounka Brooks were to join forces and purchase every media house in St. Maarten, the nature of news, the nature of journalism, the nature of the game and the players would not change.

Without some crucial challenges to the status quo, our reliance on the usual "he said, she said, he said," type of unbalanced flavor-of-the-day reporting, we'll all still be held hostage by the same limitations of language, resources, and defensive false façades that we've seemingly grown inured to. No matter who "owns" us.

Dr. Kevorkian, meet Andy
August 1998

The long arm of Johnny Law finally caught up with yours truly somewhere two hours or so outside of Portland, Oregon, today. What am I doing in Orifice? Good question. I'm supposed to be on vacation, possibly looking for a new job. But the only thing

I've vacated is my sanity, and the only thing I found was some police officers eager to get me off the road.

I was driving along not doing much of anything when I finally caught a glimpse of one of those sheriff's patrol cars zipping in behind me, simultaneously unobtrusive and invasive as hell, giving me that stomach curdling little whoop, whoop, meaning, pull over.

The officer seems like a nice guy. He tells me he's been following me for 20 miles and that he had reports that I'd narrowly missed having no fewer than six head-on collisions. Frankly, I hadn't noticed. What with jet lag, no food, no sleep, wife problems, Dutch torture and whatever else, I figure six seems too few.

After a few minutes, the real sheriff, an older guy, shows up and they ask me to perform the field sobriety tests which I fail miserably, bumbling all around looking like a spastic Jerry Lewis comedy routine. Only this is not funny. Or is it?

Naturally, I'm nervous, but I'm clean — legal if not innocent, save for a couple of prescription drugs. What I mean is I haven't consumed any alcohol or illegal substances, though the police don't seem to believe me.

They search my bag and find what I know they'll find, but they do not confiscate anything. They ask me about the Prozac and why I'm taking it. "Depressed," I say. They look at the French Valium and ask the same question. "Anxious," I say, though to them, I must appear to be underwater, my words sounding muffled, and thick.

They handcuff me and ask if I have anything in my pockets that could be used to hurt them, and despite the severity of the moment I think about Hannibal Lecter using just a paper clip to break his cuffs and then celebrate by chewing off the face of one of his capturers. All I produce from my pocket is a package of Lifesavers.

They slide me into the patrol car and bring me to the jail where I'm relieved of my Doc Martens, my belt, my watch and anything I might be able to use to kill myself. Unfortunately, they can't confiscate my brain.

A tall drug enforcement officer dressed like a cross between a SWAT team guy and a survivalist/militiaman comes by and gives me more tests and tells me my general neurological detachment leads him to think I'm either high on grass or cocaine, maybe both. He tells me I have droopy eyelids, little affect and that my pupils are strange. I mumble something about how I hope my pupils are doing well in school. I don't remember how he responded.

He asks me if I'll take a pee test and I say sure, because I have nothing much in my blood except some Prozac and the good French Valium, which when mixed together on an empty stomach has turned out to be a recipe for police attention.

The afternoon passes predictably and miserably enough. I'm booked, fingerprinted and mug shot. My info is injected into the national crime computer and there I am, a presence in criminal cyberspace.

At one point during the afternoon, the police haul in six guys who have been part of a burglary ring. I think that for a moment they might get thrown in with me, or me with them, which brings on some panic, but they're in transit, on their way upstate to Portland for processing.

Some six somewhat hazy, dehumanizing hours after all this started, I'm released from my little holding cell, and I'm given some orange juice, my Docs, my belt, my watch and court summons for October for DUI, and multiple warnings to take it easy.

Now another guy might have thanked the police for intervening and saving his life. And another guy might have seen this as the proverbial omen and gotten the message he'd been spared, and full of zeal and new resolve might have yelled to the sky in hugely overdramatic Michael Bolton, Tony Robbins or Steven Spielberg fashion "I want to live, I want to live."

I'm not that kind of guy. I'm the other guy. I take a moment to make sure no police are looking at me and then slip behind the wheel of my rented source of mobile angst and pull out of Newport rubbing my wrists where the cuffs bit, serenely following the illuminated road signs of inevitability.

Measuring Time, Measuring Loss
Reprinted from the St. Maarten Guardian, August 6, 1998

You measure the time you spend in a place not with a clock or calendar, but by the people you meet, the ones who touch your heart; the ones you've known long enough to remind you of who you once were and how you've changed.

One of those people I measure time by, a man named Glen Raguette who I have known for four years, was arrested by French Immigration police Tuesday morning at his workplace.

One way to look at it is this: Glen had been on St. Maarten/St. Martin for six years and was "undocumented" and his luck had finally run out. Glen's arrest came as a sad shock to his friends and to his co-workers who know him as a quiet, gentle, true Rasta; a man who loved Jah, Ital cooking, riding his bicycle, Reggae music, a woman named Kicki and her children: Hugo and Sophie Joy; Jenny Li, working for Red Stripe, taking very long showers, and eating mangoes picked just before dawn.

"I feel like this building just fell down on me," he said, dazed and despondent, Tuesday night at the police holding area in Concordia. He looked chilled in that way that had nothing to do with air conditioning and everything to do with shock. "I don't know what to do," he said, and he meant it.

Police, being police, will do what they want. And, any undocumented Caribbean man or woman, is fair game to these hunters. But as with most stories, there is a catch here.

The French Immigration police, for the most part, do their job effectively and humanely. There are times when they stop undocumented workers, let them go, and don't file the paperwork on them. It's discretionary, and based on a number of motives.

As one officer put it, there's a certain Haitian who gives French Police a good deal on lobsters. He manages not to get deported. French Immigration police also point to their continued frustration of arresting workers under the employ of some of St. Martin's most upstanding, influential and wealthy citizen-politicians, only to have those "illegal" workers released within an hour. This happens repeatedly.

For anyone who was shocked by the quick arrests and release of the Belvedere workers last week, events like that are apparently quite common on the French side, including the use of illegal laborers to make repairs at the Mairie. There was also a recent case concerning a St. Martin based, senior immigration police officer who was arrested for selling "papers" to illegals.

Justice is always selective, a roll of the dice, a spin of the wheel. A whim of a police officer who either likes cheap lobster or one who actually believes that an honest, good man should be allowed to slide because he is hurting no one and poses no threat to French national security.

Glen doesn't sell lobsters. His personal roulette wheel and his horoscope for the day spun wild and turned as ugly as an uncaring French police officer.

Yes, he should have made a more serious effort to get his papers, but for some reason, he never did.

Like a lot of Black men who have been hurt in ways beyond words, the details of Glen's life were uncertain, perhaps even suspicious.

I always thought he was Jamaican; turns out he was born in St. Vincent. It also could be his last name is Guy, and his age is a mystery. He had no passport, and apparently whatever other identification he had was stolen when a bag of valuables he toted with him disappeared.

And now too, he's disappeared. Floating high above the isolated tiny islands of the Caribbean, each interconnected by blood and history, but each with their own laws of entrance and expulsion, borderless yet caged. Glen was gone Wednesday to Guadeloupe along with three Haitians, and then on to Jamaica, or more hopefully, St. Vincent, where he has a sister who can help find him a birth certificate and begin the legal steps to establishing an "identity" immigration police will respect.

How do you say goodbye to a friend whose life has been yanked out from under him? You hug him and turn around, say Jah bless, listen to a door close and begin to understand that you also measure the time you spend in a place staring at asphalt and crying hot tears of helpless rage.

December 1998

I'm getting that itchy feeling which means it's time to go. The Dutch girl is expecting me to visit her in Amsterdam over Christmas. I'm supposed to leave on December 28 which would be my fifth anniversary. I know there's no way I'm going to go. I also know there's no way this anniversary will be a peaceful one. I'm free falling with no real indication that my parachute will ever open.

A funny thing about infidelity is that it colors your perception of everything; it's as if I see things with this yellowish tinge. I somehow believe that if I were Mosera, I would not be in this position. I would either have the will and self-assuredness to find my way out, or perhaps most significantly, would not have been in this situation in the first place and would have reduced all matters to a safer, more intellectualized realm. What I seem to be involved in here is a war of attrition, the same war I have been at for years and years with the only difference being others are involved. One thing remains reassuringly constant: the attritions are winning, and they show no signs of stopping till they plant their flag in the capital of my ruined soul.

Fathers and Sons
Reprinted from the St. Maarten Guardian, August 31, 1998

Many months ago my friend Ras Mosera asked me what it was I liked about the Caribbean and by extension, living in St. Martin.

I had no good nor ready answer. Part of his query I realized, was Socratic. He was helping me to learn by asking a question.

Months later I have come upon an answer, and it is a very personal one. These days, I dream a lot of my father; I think a lot about fathers and sons in general.

My father died when I was a boy. He was 38. Had he lived — his birthday was earlier this month, he would have been 67.

I am now older than my father was when he died. I have outlived my father, but not in the usual way. I buried my father and my feelings for him.

St. Maarten is a crucible, a place that tests you, especially if you are not Caribbean. It makes you remember things, feel things.
It is a paradoxical place of great beauty and tolerance, but it is also a place of unfathomably complicated emotional situations, ultra-partisan alliances and the social quirks endemic to living in a small society.
The Caribbean, St. Maarten, is full of ghosts; the ghosts of slavery and oppression, the ghosts of the martyrs, the ghosts of regional lore and mythology, the ghosts of fathers and sons.

Being an alien here can drive you to a crisis of self-recognition. I used to think a lot of people, especially whites, looked at the Caribbean as a place to escape to; to leave one life for another.

I know that to be impossible. St. Maarten, like life, has no back door.

There is something poignant about escaping to a place where you discover you can no longer run from who you are and who you are not, and what your father might have meant to you.

The ocean will tell you if you listen. At the beginning of Homer's Odyssey, the hero, Odysseus, who has fought in many wars, is sitting by the seashore and asks the question, "does any man know who is father is?" I think it is a question many men and women ask.

Was he loving? Protective? A tyrant? Was he there to show us how to be people who respect themselves and others? Was he cold and distant, but still able to put food on the table? Did he disappear into a rum bottle and never come out?

Was he full of rage and violence, or was he even more scary because he could not express rage or emotion at all? Did he stroke your hair, divorce your mother and break your heart? Did he welcome you into a world of promise, or did he spit you out like a piece of unchewed meat?

Oddly, interestingly, I don't know if these are questions I would have asked so blatantly had I not in some ways been changed by living in St. Martin, and having been exposed in varying degrees of friendship with many men my age and a bit older.

Some of these men are fathers, others are not. I would find it immensely interesting to hear what these men think of their respective fathers and sons, and how it has impacted their lives; call it my own little exploration into the male gender.

I have watched fathers and sons here; I've seen some brutality and I've seen much love; the passing of male kindness from one generation to the next. I've seen neglect and crude affection that is sometimes hard to distinguish from abuse.

I've seen things that at first troubled and puzzled me, like men having children with multiple women. I was self-righteous about it, but I claim no moral high ground now. Now I just wonder if those children will know and love their fathers, and if these fathers will be present for those children.

Or, will some of these children, and because of gender identification, I'm thinking more about males, grow up feeling rejected by these fathers who do not recognize them. Will they, as teens, internalize that paternal vacuum and feeling of rejection and attempt to numb the pain by exhibiting angry, risk taking behavior, by using drugs, and alcohol and by falling victim to depression?

In Zen Buddhism, the learned say the ultimate goal is to give birth to one's self. Perhaps as men who are no longer as young as we once were, we must learn at some age to be our own fathers, to heal our souls, especially if we have been bereft of the real thing. I am a child of fire, born under the sign of Aries who is living on an island born from a volcano, molten fire surrounded by an ocean which cools the heat and makes forgiveness possible, however dangerous.

My father was also born under the sign of fire, a Leo. In my recent dreams I walk through the heat of a burning childhood and stare at him.

The fire burns hot, and only one of us lives to tell the story of what we know; tells it to the sand, and palm trees and Caribbean Sea that may one day grant us both, father and son, the grace to forgive.

Summer, 1997

I really like Beryl Parker Hazel, the leader of the local senior citizens group. She's got a lot of heart and she's funny and smart as they come. She always gives me a big hug and asks about Jenny Li, my wife. She's been trying seemingly forever to have a senior citizens center built on St. Maarten. They've come close to realizing their dream, but some huge wad of red tape or politics always spoils it for them. Time is very much of the essence because many of them, like Beryl, are well into their 70's

She's involved in a court case against former Lt. Gov. Russell Voges who has been living in a house owned by Beryl but not paying any rent, even though I believe his rent money comes from the government.

This is pretty par for the course in St. Maarten where people will try to get away with not paying for as long as they can, and where money floats around from hand-to-hand without ever touching down in anyone's pocket or bank account for more than a few minutes before it's on the fly again.

Voges owes her something like $6000. Voges is being defended by his live-in-lover, Elvia Moenir-Alam, with whom he reputedly has had huge, knock down, drag-out fights fueled by alcohol.

Judging from what's going on in the courthouse, Voges does not have much of a case, but his legal counsel is making motions like she's defending O.J Simpson.

Beryl, who is from one of St. Maarten's real founding families, rolls her eyes at the theatrics. Later she tells me she is not feeling that well, is having trouble walking and will soon go to New York where she has an apartment, to seek medical attention. I know Beryl can take care of herself, but it pains me to see someone like Voges treat her this way. I mean Voges doesn't even belong in the same sentence as her let alone on the same island, and here he is trying to stiff the kind of St. Maartener and person he could never be.

There is no rest for the wicked.

The silence is deafening
Reprinted from the St. Maarten Guardian, August 19, 1998

For the past several months *The Guardian* has carried a number of articles about Caribe Waste Technologies Inc. (CWT) and its plans to build a solid waste disposal facility using an essentially untested technology called Thermoselect, a gasification system that burns all types of garbage with no presorting.

While CWT executive Francis Campbell is disputing the $87 million cost of the facility, it appears the island government would have to pay roughly $4.4 million a year over 20 to 25 years. Money issues aside, there is the very real argument whether this type of sophisticated, untested solid waste facility is appropriate for St. Maarten. CWT has not adequately proven that its gasification process and subsequent "scrubbing" and cleaning processes will not produce dioxins, a family of toxins that are carcinogenic byproducts of certain incinerated materials mixed together.

Beyond the cost and possible health risks, what is astounding is that not one so-called "activist," those who yelled bloody murder about the monopolization of the media, the destruction of the lagoon, who railed against the dangers of the turnover tax, or the racism of the Franco-Dutch Treaty, has said a word about this.

Let's face it, a solid waste disposal plant is just not a "sexy" issue.

Commissioner William Marlin was cited last week as saying he will sign the letter of intent on the project.

Before the CWT deal does go through, and a lot rides on what happens with GEBE, which CWT has offered to operate, a lot of questions have not yet been posited.

Is this proposed plant safe enough to construct in a residential area? Will people have to be relocated, and if so, where? What happens if St. Maarten cannot meet the projected quota of 300 tons of garbage per day? Will refuse have to be imported in order to keep the price of $4.4 million fixed? What if CWT does not find a buyer in the United States for the residual, vitrified materials?

Do you want a gasification plant and some mercury a couple of hundred yards from your back yard? Has the CWT feasibility report been sent to the environmental consultants TNO in Holland, and if it has, what were the recommendations and/or problems with it?

The silence from elected public officials and "activists" about the CWT deal is disturbing and hypocritical. Why, with the signing of the letter of intent so close and the deal an apparent *fait accompli* has the opposition only now called for an "urgent" meeting of the Island Council?

It should have happened much earlier. With all the loud and persistent talk about the future of the island resting in the lauded hands of "our youth", shouldn't the public be fully apprised of all the potential risks this waste-to-energy plant might present to the environmental and economic future of St. Maarten?

Everyone agrees the Pondfill dump is an eyesore, unhealthy and potentially carcinogenic in its own right. It has to be replaced, and transformed. But is the CWT facility the most appropriate, cost-efficient way to solve the island's solid waste problems? Is environmental safety being shortcut for expedience and profit? Why have other, less expensive plans been ignored or dismissed?

By right, voices should have been raised by now - many of them - and questions asked about all facets of this deal. But there's been nothing, only written words tumbling one after the other into a vacuum of apparent apathy; the silence is deafening.

No offense, but you're fucked in the head, right?
November, 1998

Almost got into a fight today with Marvin Dollison, also known as "King Stunky," the fire fighter. He thinks I write only negative things about his beloved St. Maarten Patriotic Alliance, and nothing bad about the Democratic Party. I always thought of myself as an equal opportunity sniper, which is not saying much, because there is little to choose from ideologically between the SPA and the DP. The SPA is blacker and long-suffering because the DP under alcohol-loving and crooked white ruler Claude Wathey ran the island for 30 years, enough time to rip off land, sell the island's soul for the proverbial pieces of silver, get rich and turn a one-time Eden into a real Pimper's Paradise.

I think the only thing the SPA really objects to is that they did not get the chance to do it first. The SPA is used to being the opposition, and when they finally got into government they still had that defensive, us against the world mentality.

The DP is lighter skinned, full of hard drinkers and the shrill light-skinned women who marry them, and playboys running money making schemes usually in the form of hawking particular products, like gasoline, auto parts, gas stations, real estate and so on. Both parties are deeply attached and indebted to the island's rich guys, some of whom own Mafia casinos and hotels. Both parties have arrogant politicians in positions of huge conflict of interest whereby their companies, businesses and friends are profiting greatly from favors and contracts awarded by politicians.

So, besides the race issue, and the reality that the SPA is in government and is doing exactly what the DP would do if they were in, there's little to choose from. But Stunky is becoming obsessed with this.

I'm beginning to think that Stunky, like his fellow Dollisons, Raffie and Domingo, is fucked in the head. Esther and Germina told me that Raffie's mother is crazy and used to drop the baby Raffie on his head. Domingo more or less lives on the streets, but he has a regular if part-time job of taking down the flags in front of the Government Building and police station at 6 p.m. each evening.

Stunky is marginally better, brighter and more presentable than Raffie and Domingo, but louder and nastier too.

He yells at me in the streets that he's going to have me deported, that my days are numbered. Meanwhile, I'm trying to keep myself together, I'm depressed and it's taking hold like a toothache that never goes away. My head feels as crowded as one of those tenement buildings with 24 people living in three rooms. I skulk through the streets hoping to avoid any and all human contact, because I just can't take it anymore. One more stare, one more meaningless good morning, one more anything.

But there's Stunky calling me out like a big parrot in front of a fire engine till finally I go over to him and tell him if he wants a piece of me to go ahead, I'm just dying to file a police report against him, so take a shot, or otherwise write a letter to the editor of the Guardian, but in any event, just shut the fuck up. It's tense for a few seconds. Stunky is surrounded by his colleagues. I have no doubt he wants to hit me, but he stays in control, nothing happens and I walk away. This time.

October 1998

Occasionally I hang out at the Hong Kong restaurant, a couple of streets down from the Guardian and one of the best places to check out the ever-fascinating interactions between St. Maarteners and the Chinese who serve them.

The Hong Kong gets a lot of guys from the GEBE, the local electricity provider, who come in and drink during the afternoons. I'm sitting there one day and I watch a St. Maarten-Curaçao clone, fortified by his three staples, Heineken, Marlboros and a Rolex watch, grab the thin arm of a tiny but pregnant waitress and tell her, "hey, Chinee girl, where my chicken leg... hey, you wan' come home with me, Chinee girl and have a real man?"

She wriggles free, his fingerprints on her arm and the guys he's with just laugh and laugh, while meanwhile, at a table under a big TV that is never turned off and always plays Chinese videos, a group of restaurant employees eat fast and ferociously talking in firecracker Chinese as the GEBE guys get louder and looser and keep calling for the "Chinee girl" to bring them their food, hot.

I have this feeling that while the Chinese might be impassive in public and ignore indignities like being called "Chinee" girl and China man, back in the kitchen one of the cooks, those small thin guys who work 20 hours a day, is spitting a big loogie laced with TB or whatever else he has into the freshly woked stewed dog he's ready to serve up to the gracious and waiting St. Maarten public.

I don't doubt this because a few weeks ago, there were at least six stray dogs hanging around the Hong Kong dumpster, and now they're gone, and you can bet your next plate of Moo Goo Gai Mutt, they haven't been adopted.

Min and Reggie, a love story

"Do you know how sad you make me feel when you look at me like that," the dying man said with a sweet smile, his big bear paw swallowing her little hand like a gumdrop.

"I love you," the man said.

"You're a fool," she said, but she put her hand on his and moved it back and forth as if trying to erase something.

"I love you," the bear said again.

"Which means you're still a fool. And me too."

Min met Reggie twenty three years before the government fell and the island was renamed. Min was from Hong Kong, born during a time when a great few had much wealth, and everyone else had varying degrees of nothing. Min's family fell into this latter category.

So, when she was sixteen, her father gave her a choice: I will sell you in marriage and you can stay close to home, or you can accept passage to the Caribbean and work in the cousin's business.

And so, Min came to the island and soon found herself working sixteen hours a day at the Pink Pagoda, the bar-restaurant owned by her cousin Tien Yok.

After just a few months, Min knew she wanted out. The grease and smoke smells were making her sick; she could not look at another piece of pork, rice kernel or cigarette butt floating in sickly soup without thinking, "I am dying here one second at a time."

Which led her to Reggie. Min had to get out, but there was the rather sticky problem of the rather large sum of money she'd have to pay Tien Yok to buy her freedom.

Min knew that Tien Yok owned her, even if they called it "sponsorship". He owned her for the sixteen hours a day she worked and he owned her when she slept, because awake or asleep, all Min could think about was either sticking a knife in Tien Yok's heart or one in her own. Either way, she was going to get out.

And there was Reggie. Big, fat, nice, rich Reggie. Little bit sad Reggie. Smart also, surprising. One time he spoke to her in halting but correct Cantonese, saying something like "I would like a lovely beer." She laughed, astonished to hear this brown fellow speak Chinese.

"Picked up some traveling after Korea, the war," he told her, the beer bottle disappearing into the impossible folds of those big paws. Big, soft panda she thought, always quiet, polite, never drunk.

One day, she put it to him.

"Please, show me what it's like to be from here. Help me. Teach me to be like you."

She wasn't stupid. She expected it to be a transaction and she took stock of what she had, youth, dark, thick hair, a nice enough face and breasts that would disappear in his hands.

"Please."

He didn't say anything at first. Just considered her gravely like a big bear afraid of both the bees and the honey. All he said was "all right."

An agreement was worked out between Tien Yok and Reggie, and Min came into Reggie's house and business.

To some, it seemed an odd arrangement. Reggie had his wife Maria of twenty years who he loved but no longer liked and who no longer spoke to him.

At night, after working the day beside Reggie in his hardware store and grocery, Min would hear the TV playing in Maria's room and would fall asleep to voices that belonged to no one.

This is how it went for more than two decades. Reggie taught Min the best he could how to be from the island, tried to give her what she would need to know. He never touched her; he didn't think she'd need to know that, or even want it. Truth is, he loved her like a daughter because that was all he could do, and that was the most pure kind of love he could think of, the most honorable.

And for Min, Reggie was the earth, the air, the moon, the sky. Her life.

Min had had but two lovers in her life. The first ground into her so hard she felt she was something between the mortar and the pestle. The second was like looking in the mirror, the same breasts, mounds and canyons. It was too much like being alone.

Right before the trouble began with the burnings on Frontstreet and all the Indian people were forced to leave the island after the nationalists drove them out, Reggie lost his appetite, which was cause for worry because he loved his food and beer, and now he wanted neither.

He sat on the porch and complained of a dull ache in his groin and back; saw ravens everywhere and began to cry, the tears moving down his face like it was melting, creasing his cheek and dropping in small pools on his folded paws.

And so, Min climbed into Reggie's bed and hugged what was left of his once great belly, hugged it like it was her unborn child. Nursed it. She made a den for him there, cleaning him up, feeding him when he could eat, holding his hand tightly, as if memorizing his fingerprints.

"The fuck what people will say," Min said to herself, the sound of Maria's TV coming through the wall, the sound of someone laughing on Wheel of Fortune.

When Reggie went, scared and alone, when he asked if she had love for him and breathed his last breath into her mouth, Min smoothed his brow and closed his eyes, got up, walked across the hall, went into Maria's room, walked past the old sleeping woman and turned off the TV.

She went back to Reggie, eased him out of his diaper so no one would see him that way in the morning and wrapped herself around him, kissing him like she was trying to eat an ice cream before it all melted; wrapped around him, a middle-aged woman hugging a teddy bear.

Her days now are the long arc of the sun in the shack she lives in in the Chinese Quarter. Many of the Chinese, like the Indians, fled when faced with dealing with the nationalists, but not Min. Reggie had taught her to be from here.

One morning, she watched an odd sight, two people running up the beach beside her house. Odd, because there was no fishing anymore, and not many people came by here.

But there was a girl, maybe 17, followed by a tall man with dreadlocks. Min sensed they were father and daughter, the older running behind the younger giving her room to stretch like a colt, but keeping a close eye on her. Their movements were so similar, so in concert, that Min felt she was watching two dancers. The girl came toward Min and smiled, then suddenly, she grimaced and looked fierce. Min was frightened at first, but then realized the father was gaining on the girl and the girl refused to be caught and passed.

The man ran by Min and grinned beatifically as his daughter bolted ahead flying toward the sea. Min watched them, chasing each other running and running and running till there was nowhere left to run.

Portrait for portrait
November 1997

Notary at law and longtime Dutch-born, St. Maarten resident, Jose Speetjens came up with a really interesting proposition. Speetjens, who knows where all the bones are buried on this island, commissioned Mosera, the island's most accomplished and daring artist, and Cynric Griffith, who might be the best portrait painter on St. Maarten, to paint portraits of each other.

It's intriguing, not only because it's very unusual to have a patron of the arts here, but because the two artists, at least superficially, are very different.

Cynric is in his 60's, which makes him a good 20 years older than Mosera. Also, Cynric is a meticulous, contained painter who studied art in New York. Though sensitive, he's a traditionalist.

If Griffith is the keeper of the flame, then Mosera is the fire. A couple of months ago, he unveiled a new series of paintings called Placebo, in which he blazes new ground, far more sexual, angry and overtly mythological than anything shown before on St. Maarten.

I got a look at the two paintings at Mosera's gallery today and true to his keen sense of form, Griffith rendered Mosera in a naturalistic way that captured the younger artist in brownish hues, regal and handsome, yet somehow burdened by expectation or fatigue.

Likewise, the expressionistic Mosera captured the contained, yet distracted energy that surrounds Cynric, his guarded dignity. I did a pretty long story in the Guardian about the portrait for portrait that both artists seemed to like, which I found gratifying. The more I sat with each artist and spoke with them, the more I began to recognize their similarities. Both men have been creating since they were children. Mosera recalled sitting in the St. Lucian sun as a child making mudcake creatures, soaked in sweat and risking ridicule to do what he knew felt right.

Griffith told me that when he was five years old he used the clean white sheets his mother hung out to dry in the warm St. Kitts' air as a makeshift canvas, thus making his mother his first, and most direct art critic. Doing a story like this reminds me how much I like writing about art, and in this case, actually writing about two men of accomplishment who place talent, craft and creativity above all else. Two faces with a view, a portrait of the artist by the artist, nice idea Mr. Speetjens.

By the way, the office of notary is an important one on St. Maarten. A notary does much work with deeds and contracts, and is appointed by the "queen." Speetjens is a quiet notary. The other big notary in town, Elco Rosario, is a not quiet notary, but loves to stir the shit and who despite his charm and exuberance, is more often than not getting his balls broken by Dutch investigators for one thing or another.

Not so for quiet Speetjens, gentleman farmer, art patron, and very, very wealthy man. Now, if I could only get him to let me write about where all those bones are buried.

Mosera: I want to shock
Reprinted from the St. Maarten Guardian, September 12, 1997

There is no turning back now for Ras Mosera, and why should there be? In his new series of paintings, which will officially be on view this weekend at Mosera's Fine Arts Gallery on Frontstreet, he has left one artistic nation for another; gone flying.

He has leaped the boundary like an Olympic hurdler holding a paint brush, with a passport stamped "no longer necessary", and taken off for an artistic landscape that is wilder, more political, darkly sexual and far angrier than the one he left behind.

In other words, sorry Roland Richardson, you can chop down that flamboyant tree, baby, because the face of art is cha-cha-changing.

Ironically, the collection of 15 works,

some of them very provocative, large pieces with rusty-coppery-colored backgrounds, bears the name "Placebo," which is also the name of an individual painting, which is the centerpiece of this unique offering.

The painting, which is not a placebo, but in many ways a bitter pill of recognition, is a representation of spiritual, yet priapic numbness brought on by the false riches and sensual gratifications of living in a high-buzz colonial haze.

It is a definite eye-opener and an indication that Mosera is thinking in terms of "statement" paintings that depict not only a scene but the ethos of a pained people. It could be seen as his "Guernica," the amazing and enraged huge work Pablo Picasso fired off in a genius response to fascism and Francoism in Spain.

"Placebo," the painting, because it is graphic in its depiction of an unsettling figure complete with gaudy wristwatch, and erect penis, was at first denied a place the "Six Visions of Paradise" exhibition in Curaçao.

The painting will be hung at the exhibition, but another Mosera work on display at his gallery, "The Zulu Look," will be in the official catalogue rather than the more controversial "Placebo," which depicts the psychosexual shackles of colonial consumerism.

"It's about the rush we get from colonialism and how we sugarcoat ourselves with brand names and materialism", Mosera said. "I wanted something deeper."

The seeds for this startling new direction were sown in Santo Domingo about a year ago. According to Mosera, he was part of the Netherlands Antilles contingent at the Biennal Expo.

"I thought the art was too comfortable, not confrontational," Mosera said Thursday, while preparing for Saturday's opening. "I just felt in the Caribbean sense, there were no 'household' paintings," he continued, alluding to immortal signature works from Europe that were immediately recognizable and went far beyond the safe and decorative.

Looking at "Placebo," which features the word "imported" spelled out in Hindi, Chinese, Dutch and other languages, Mosera said, "some will say they are shocked. I want to shock. I want a reaction."

Much of the new work, beyond being defiant, is also quirky and humorous. There is a painting that depicts a man picking his nose that is oddly comical and tragic at the same time. Mosera, who has always used mythological references in his work, does so to the extreme in a painting depicting a strikingly sexual woman slaying a minotaur. The painting bears a sly trademark which reads, "new mythology."

"Somebody told me they thought it was the killing of colonialism," he said, "to destroy the old mythology to create new myths."

Interestingly, the painting "Visa," inspired by Mosera's travails in trying to obtain a U.S. visa, and what that process said about the dehumanization of a people defined by passport, boundary and language, has yet to be officially unveiled in St. Maarten. After being on exhibit in Cuba, the work is now being shown in Sweden.

Art is a world without boundaries, without compromise. Great artists fire bullets, but give you the time to duck while you watch them hit their intended target; Mosera, your aim is true.

"If you wish to drown, do not torture yourself with shallow water."
Bulgarian Proverb

October 1997

As I get older my capacity for verbal cruelty and uncoolness astounds me. It's not that I mean to be testy, it's just that when I'm stressed, I forget how to act any other way. I'm not on edge all the time, just most of it.

There just happen to be certain times, often when I have to swallow a lot of bullshit or shine up some asshole who couldn't find his way out of a phone booth, that I go into overdrive.

Take this guy I'll call Adrian R., yet another bawnhere who went to Holland and studied something in college, in his case theater arts, who returns home, and wants St. Maarten to know he's back and ready to contribute to his little island. How does he let them know? By setting up an interview for himself in the newspaper whereby he talks about himself and what he has planned and what he can offer the public. He can't say much of what he's done, because he hasn't done anything. And he can't say much of what he really plans to do because it's still "preliminary."

At moments like this I feel like a job counselor or something, rather than a journalist. Finally, I asked the guy if he thought there was anything particularly newsworthy about his being back, and whether he felt he could do a better job than Ian Valz, the longtime drama director.

He flares and tells me, "I hope you're aware you subconsciously favor Ian Valz." First of all, I didn't know there was any real issue between the two to speak of, I was just fishing around. And secondly, if my preference was subconscious, how could I be aware of it?

Amazingly, against my better judgment, I write a little puff piece that says nothing more than "A-drain" is back. More amazingly, the next day, the guy phones me up to complain of a typo. Complaining about a typo in the Guardian is like saying the ocean is a little too salty.

I listen patiently for about six seconds and then tell him I not only didn't give a fuck about what he said yesterday, I give less of a fuck now.

He starts to say something about how he's the future of St. Maarten and how I'm just what I am but I've already hung up.

The Gold Standard

Been seeing a lot of kids wearing gold lately. I mean real little kids, less than a year old wearing little gold bracelets, chains and earrings. It's a status thing I know, but it has to mess up a kid's body chemistry wearing all that gold when they're not yet completed beings. This one little boy, perhaps two, was decked out in enough gold to make your average Curaçao man suck his teeth in envy.

The kid had an earring, bracelet, neck chain and little ring on his chubby finger. All he was missing was a mini-Rolex watch. You get started on gold too early and maybe you get hooked on it and always crave more, a junkie for precious metal and the money to buy it.

"Ich Bin Ein St. Maartner" (or Bruno and Heidi Love SXM Carnival) Reprinted from the St. Maarten Guardian, April 28, 1998

Bruno and Heidi love Carnival. Until last Wednesday night, they weren't even sure what Carnival was, but now they know.

Bruno and Heidi are from Germany, a country not exactly known for its sense of humor, living sweetness, or spontaneity.

They heard about Carnival at the large ITB show in Berlin earlier this year, you know, the one attended by the Commissioner of travel, er tourism, Julian Rollocks, and decided to sink their Deutschmarks in a trip to St. Maarten for Mas.

Now, Bruno and Heidi have been around. After completing their undergraduate studies at the University of Heidelberg, they ran with the bulls in Pamplona, visited the Hagia Sophia in Istanbul, went whitewater rafting in Colorado and climbed Mt. Scenery in Saba.

They mourned the death of the great Austrian techno-disco-rocker Falco in the Dominican Republic two months ago, and then suffered silently at home when they learned that one of the two guys who comprised Milli-Vanilli had committed suicide.

But none of these real-life experiences prepared them for St. Maarten's 29th edition of Carnival. First there was the T-shirt Jump Up where some young men got so caught up in the spirit that they pulled their pants down, way down. The Full Monty. Heidi's pallor at that point went from Snow White to Red Rat in a matter of Milli-Vanilli- seconds. As for Bruno, he kept the video cam running.

But Heidi and Bruno hadn't seen anything till they ventured into the Carnival Village last Wednesday to catch the all local show, "Tis We own T'in."

The Teutonic twosome took in Fernando Clark, bouncing around the stage like a football; they saw numerous singers, dancers, and cavorters, including their favorite commissioner, Rollocks, who was trapped by three women like he was wearing flesh overcoats. And finally, a closing act by King Timo, that caused Bruno to exclaim, "mein gott, dis is raw. So verrrry ethnic. Mein landsmen in Shermany vould love dis. I vonder how can I export Carnival to Shermany?"

Bruno looked over at Heidi who apparently was in shock. But this did not deter Bruno, who at 4:15 a.m., and on his 23rd Red Stripe, had his pants up but his cultural guard down and proclaimed, "I have seen the Carnival light. I vill export Carnival to Deutschland. Ich bin ein St. Maartener."

A few hours later when Heidi had recovered, and Bruno had told her of his plans, she reminded him that there were some logistical problems to overcome. For one thing, she pointed out, "vee Shermans do not know how to yam, or get down for that matter. Remember Bruno, vee are not terribly comfortable doing our own ding. Vee tend to follow the pack."

Bruno told her this might have been true once, but that Germans were changing and they could indeed, jam, bam, ram, and if necessary, cram. Bruno said he would solve this problem with a Carnival starter kit so that shy Germans could practice alone, in the privacy of their homes and perfect their Carnival attitudes.

"First thing, vee will play our Rolling Tones, King Beau Beau and Timo CD's so zat vee too vill be raw Socamatic reveling machines. Yah Heidi? Vee vill play, vee vill dance und vee vill spread the vord."

Heidi pointed out that no Carnival starter kit would be complete without Fernando Clark. "Hafter all, Bruno, he seems to be every place at once. Introducing, telling yokes, making funny mit der Commissar Rollocks."

"Yah, yah, Heidi. Absolutely right, vee must include Fernando Clark."

Their discussions went on this way for the remainder of their vacation, through the Carnival Queen and Calypso King Shows, and Children's Parade, all the while making plans for Carnival in Germany and figuring out how to get everything just right, including Jouvert.

Finally, it struck Bruno that something was missing. "Heidi, I don't know vat it is. But something is lacking. Vee haf all the pieces but somehow it does not make a hole." "Yah, yah, Bruno, you are right," Heidi said. "Vee cannot duplicate the sweat, the soul, the animus that goes into it."

"Vus is animus," asked a puzzled Bruno.

"Vell, perhaps you are right. It is not like the St. Maarteners vill dress up in lederhosen and dance around during Octoberfest."

"Not likely," Heidi said. "Just so," Bruno sighed, adding, "still, vee vill always have our memories."

"Yah," said Heidi, "und our videotapes."

February 1998

The Island Council results are in and no surprise, Theo Heyliger, star of the Democratic Party, won big, garnering the most votes by far. The fact that his grandfather Claude Wathey, the big boss and co-founder of the DP, died just a few weeks ago, didn't hurt, neither did all the money the candidate poured into the election.

It doesn't take much to run for office in St. Maarten. I think you can even be a convicted felon and run for office.

Just a couple of signatures and you can join a "list", which is not the same as a political party because there are no provisions for political parties in the Netherlands Antilles, although politicians and journalists refer to lists as parties. Confusing enough?

The elections are not democratic in the sense that a candidate with as few as 70 votes can gain a seat on the Island Council as long as his "list" is dominant.

My favorite candidate in this year's Island Council elections was Calvin York, the number four candidate on the list of the NEMAN. He's my nominee for the most selfless, not to mention invisible candidate. York received exactly zero votes, which means obviously, he did not even vote for himself. Give him credit for good judgment.

The quit while you're behind award definitely has to go Peter Gunn born Peter Gonsalves, the racist and none-too-bright leader of the Conservative Democratic Party. Railing on about communism, deportations of non-Antilleans, capital punishment and other right wing notions, Gunn was among the first to beat the electoral bushes months before anyone else was thinking about the elections. They must have been the wrong bushes. He got 22 votes.

November 1997

I've got to give thanks that St. Maarteners, especially the politicians, have not shown any interest in human cloning. That's it.

Journey Between Zen and Now
Reprinted from the St. Maarten Guardian, April 6, 1998

I was feverishly working my fingers over the dial, navigating the radio stations of infinity, trying to tune in to Radio Free St. Martin, when it happened.

The voice was soothing, with a trace of a Far East accent — Bruce Lee, Byron Lee, Spike Lee?

"This is Roshi Richardson-Gumbs, and this is Zen Radio," he said. "The approach is spiritual, uncluttered, a bit enigmatic and challenging, for it is not the same to speak of bulls as to be in the bullring, is it? We can talk about anything you like. Remember, the best moment is now, when things are what they seem to be, as if you were seeing them for the first time. Ask me questions and my answers will convey the essence of Zen."

First caller. Welcome.

"Yes. I had a question about the Carnival '98 poster. It scares me and my children. All the women look like men and the colors are nightmarish, garish."

"To that I must refer you to Oscar Wilde who said, 'It is only shallow people who do not judge by appearances.'"

"I think I understand, but I'm still scared."

"Caller, ponder this Zen Koan. It will relax you: What is your original face before your mother and father were born?"

Next caller, welcome.

"Brother Roshi. This is the Cowboy. I'd like to know why no repairs have been made to the sewage lines in my area, and why the island government is trying to disrespect me."

"Dear Cowboy, I invoke the Zen saying, 'catch the vigorous horse of your mind.' As for the part of the government, ruminate on this saying by Zen scholar Alan Watts: 'No one's mouth is big enough to utter the whole thing.'"

Listeners, this next call comes from Philipsburg.

"Good afternoon, Mr. Zen-Gumbs. I'm troubled about my status in the Twilight Zone of civil servants. How can I find meaning in the workplace?"

"Dear child of twilight, you have a flare for the dramatic, and thus, I refer you to a dramatist. It was Bertold Brecht who asked, 'what happens to the hole when the cheese is gone?'"

We have another caller on the line.

"I am of the clergy, and every year, about this time, I fret about Carnival and its negative impact on my congregation, especially the men and the children. I fear this year may be worse than ever."

"Oh learned mas clergy. I will direct you to a Zen-like saying by the late American humorist Lenny Bruce. 'Everyday people are straying away from church and going back to God.' If that is not enough, think about this: 'Water which is too pure has no fish.'"

Next caller, you are on the line.

"I'm a politician and I can't seem to talk about anything but the harbor development project. It's not my fault. I'm constantly asked questions about it and I go into ever-expanding details and my eyes glaze over, and their eyes glaze over and, and, and..."

"And kindly politician, some clarity, some

uncluttered calm is called for, is it not? I refer you to Nietzsche who said, 'If you gaze for long into the abyss, the abyss also gazes into you.'"

My engineer tells me our next caller is on a car phone in St. Peters.

"Yes, I'm a former senator, and I, well, I need a job now, or at least for 11 months until one of my replacements gives me back my seat. I need something to do."

"Former senator, too often we define ourselves by our jobs, our public face. The great psychoanalytic thinker Erich Fromm observed, "man's main task in life is to give birth to himself."

"Uh well, Roshi, I'm not so sure about that."

"Then think of it this way my good DP friend. 'Every exit is an entry somewhere else.'"

It was about now that I decided to turn the dial, before I found myself trying to describe the sound of one hand clapping. I was afraid my tenuous grasp of reality was finally going to give out. I found another station.

A caller from Middle Region was asking Lloyd Richardson, the dean of talk show hosts and one not prone to heavy philosophical lifting on the air, if he thought Vance James would form a new party. That's more like it, I thought, both relieved and anxious.

Lloyd pondered and answered, "caller, I have to refer you to Basho, who said, 'Do not seek to follow in the footsteps of the men of old; seek what they sought.'"

Et tu Lloyd? My mouth dropped open. To quote Red Rat, "oh no, this is serious," everybody's beginning to sound like a Zen master.

So I called up Roshi and told him of my plight, my journey between Zen and now, of the forest and the trees.

He mulled it over, and I'm sure he said, "in your case, this applies. 'Ultimately, the marksman aims at himself.'"

Charles bows out
November 1998

Charles Borromeo Hodge killed himself on Saturday night near his neat little house beside the Fresh Pond. He took a small handgun, put it to his head and pulled the trigger. I can say I was both shocked and unsurprised at the news. Charles had just published his first book of poetry with the House of Nehesi. It was full of his overblown, wordy rhyme, some of which I think was plagiarized directly from Keats and Tennyson.

Charles was a real soldier of words, but he was no poet. The late James Dickey said poetry occurs when the utmost reality and the utmost strangeness coincide. In his devotion to form and rhyme, Charles took no risks with language or meter. He repeated rather than invented. At Charles' book party in June, always a very indulgent and rather flatulent gathering of the House of Nehesi regulars, Michel Chance, the editor of the Chronicle, compared Charles to his idol, the Jamaican poet Claude McKay. Charles was no McKay. Reading Charles was akin to following one of those arching vaults in vast medieval churches that lead the eye to stained glass but not to heaven.

But that kind of critique seems trivial and mean now. Fact is Charles was a passionate and intelligent man, if eccentric and troubled as well.

More than anything else, Charles loved big women. By big, I mean muy grande. He had a fetish about them and wrote about them like a tender pornographer. I sometimes preedited some of his work for the Guardian (he was a regular contributor) and I'll tell you, Charles wrote with a dictionary and thesaurus at his side. Even his soft porn featured polysyllabic and arcane words.

I reviewed Charles' book recently and questioned whether or not he was really a poet. Yet I didn't really come down hard on him because in many ways I liked him, and unlike many St. Maarteners, Charles was a good listener willing to exchange ideas and listen to other viewpoints.

Charles, like a lot of St. Maarteners had some very jumpy skeletons in his closet. It seems that when he was a young man, he did a lot of writing for Jose Lake Sr. who founded The Windward Islands Opinion, St. Maarten's first real newspaper. The story goes, or at least one story goes, that Charles went slightly mad after being rejected by a young woman of his dreams, and following something of a disagreement with his mentor, allegedly burned down Jose Lake's printery.

Charles spent many years in exile, living in Harlem, N.Y. and working as a postal employee. Finally, he returned to St. Maarten and began writing this odd flowery and formal poetry rife with forced rhymes that seemingly never touched on any real facet of his life.

The irony of life in general and St. Maarten in particular is that Charles' book of poems was published by Lasana Sekou, the son of Jose Lake Sr., a man Charles takes great pains to praise at every turn.

Though Charles bitched that Sekou was holding up his book for publication and spending too much time promoting the work of younger poets like Esther Gumbs and Debbie Jack, Charles seemed genuinely grateful that his Songs and Images of St. Martin would finally make it to print.

I'm sure people will talk about Charles in the days to come, and theories will sprout up about his suicide; he was unhappily in love, he was ill, he was depressed about what was happening to St. Maarten, he was suffering a letdown of sorts after the initial euphoria of publishing his book. Who knows? Maybe he was just tired and wanted to sleep forever with those big fat girls and their guitar-shaped asses.

I realize I've rambled about Charles, but somehow that's fitting. What's odd and somehow beautiful about Charles' killing himself is that it is as close as he could ever come to a poetic gesture; the linking of the fantastic and the commonplace with a single thin thread of irony: this man who loved words failed to leave a suicide note.

A Perfect Ghost
Reprinted from the St. Maarten Guardian, January 8, 1998

The avalanche of tributes, poetic hyperbole, commentaries and general hagiography as it applies to the life and times of the late Dr. Claude Wathey continues. This is no surprise. Up until his political downfall in 1993, Wathey had become synonymous with the development, growth and emergence of a "new St. Maarten", for better or for worse. But no life even when refracted in the softening shadows of death, is perfect or saintly.

Beyond the poems, the sincere and inane commentaries, including the one that likened Wathey in some respects to Dr. Martin Luther King, the talk shows, editorials and testimonials, lies the fact that a life is a complicated thing; a strange nexus of glories, bad choices, disappointments, love gained, love lost, betrayals, triumphs and simple survival.

What I know of the late Mr. Wathey came in snippets of conversation, of watching his trial in 1994, where he seemed more specter than spectacle; of talking to his sons and reading the "Claude: A Portrait of Power by Fabian Badejo". In other words, I profess no level of intimacy nor expertise on the life of

Mr. Wathey.

But at the risk of heresy, it seems what is lacking in this understandably emotional postmortem view of Claude Wathey is a sense of balance. Though power can be achieved without bloodletting, it is never a victimless procedure. For every person Claude enriched, "financially empowered" and nurtured, there were also many who felt his scorn and the wrath of opposing a hardline political ruler who did not take kindly to dissenting opinions. One thing sticks in my mind. It is Leo Friday talking about how people had to hide in alleys to read the Windward Islands Opinion published by the dissident and journalist Joseph Lake Sr. How Lake Sr. was spat upon for his political views and how he suffered for his opposition.

I differ from those who understand in some innate way, what Wathey represented in terms of the ethos of this part of the island, of the kind of pride he instilled in an elevated standard of living through the development of tourism and the influx of unprecedented capital and material goods.

But who is to say the growth did not come as some kind of Faustian bargain?A piece of your soul for a pocket of silver. A system based on patronage, largess, intimidation and toeing the line.

In the book the "Great Gatsby" by F. Scott Fitzgerald, the narrator, Nick Carroway looks across the Long Island Sound and sees the great lawns of Jay Gatsby, the strange light emanating there, the voices "that sound like money". Nick is wooed by the visions and by Gatsby; ultimately rejects it as he watches Gatsby's destruction, but never rejects Gatsby's adherence to the dream and pursuit of the mystery of the great vision of his own becoming. It's a stretch, but that's a little how Claude comes across —your vision defines you even after it undoes you. We sometimes pay a hellish price for escorting our dreams to reality.

There was much ado on the radio Tuesday concerning Claude's wishes to be cremated, not to have a large funeral, a perfect venue for people to make political hay at his expense and exercise their rights to be hypocrites. It was an elegant and intelligent last wish, one his family obeyed, and one that should have been left alone by others, but wasn't, both for the political and unseemly attention-getting plays that Wathey apparently wished to avoid in the first place.

Look at it this way, a man lives a certain number of years, absorbs the slings and arrows of outrageous fortune, watches his body succumb to the ravages of time and illness, and makes a final wish to leave that body. Ashes to ashes, dust to dust...

And so it is fitting that even in his death Wathey remains a Gatsby-like character, one people talk about, cast as villain and victim, and helplessly try to grasp, puzzled by the futility of catching smoke. One who invented himself, intrigued, intimidated, charmed, fooled and inspired others, and continues to define himself in death; a perfect ghost.

La Brea
January, 1998

I know I whine incessantly about St. Maarten, and I have tried to leave, but I return, like some hard luck salmon swimming up the wrong river. It seems I'm not through auditioning for hell quite yet. I think it's all some childhood thing, some need to be punished, or self-punished, some need for self-abnegation, some reminder of the incredible insensitivities and abuses one suffers, that leads like a plumb line to childhood. I've had conversations with Mosera about humility as a way of life, being humble before man and god. I am not a humble person. This is not to say I'm a braggart or boastful or anything like that. Quite the opposite. I learned early on from my father that my life would be a fragmentary thing, my reflection fleeting from a broken mirror, never whole.

Being humble is easy if you've never been humiliated. But if most of your life has been as tinged with the stain of humiliation as mine has, it's impossible.

I don't like to fall into the trap of blaming everything on childhood experience and trauma, but one event in my life changed me forever.

I remember my father and I were in a bathhouse, a changing room at a lake, and he kept smacking me. It was a methodical kind of beating, slow, meant more to torture and intimidate than to injure. It seemed to go on forever, all the while, my father was in various states of disrobing— the pants come off, boom, I'm hit in the back. The dick appears out of the undies, and boom, I'm slapped in the shoulders. I don't know how long this Oedipal videotape for the sadistic lasted. What I do remember is that there must have been at least a dozen male adults in the room, including one guy and his son who had come along with my father on this visiting day for lost souls, and not one of them interceded, not one of them tried to help me.

I was seven years old the summer that happened and quite simply, I never trusted anyone ever again. I still don't. No one. It's probably doomed me. I have no real connection to any other human being. That's not exactly true. I have them, I just don't feel them. I watch them hover around me like junked satellites and I have no idea of whether I'm missing out on something, heavenly signals, or just avoiding the inescapable conclusion that all human relationships, all interactions are ultimately unsatisfying and condemned to a ragged orbit.

My total defeatism and fatalism is in ironic counterpoint to a culture in which so many others of my generation seek healing and grace in aging and experience. They exhaust crystals, philosophies, 12-step groups, counseling, diet and herbal remedies in pursuit of "healing."

I see no healing for me. I'm a hemophiliac in a razor blade factory; I'm marking red, streaky time.

Luckily, I can see the whole process from every side imaginable: victim and victimizer; abused and abuser, junkie and enabler.In my world, this is what passes for perspective.

I used to worry that I would turn out like my father, but I don't anymore. His being would loom over me when I felt violent towards my wife; either hurt or misunderstood by something she said, or totally dismissed and moved almost to the point of no-return to hit her just to silence that tone that flags my rage like a red cape.

In my heart, I may be worse than my father. I'm a killer. I'm an emotional pickpocket who knows how to hurt and can do with surprisingly little remorse.

But I'm not him. Despite my moral flexibility, I've drawn lines. I do not practice the vulgarity of his obvious violence. Instead, I've perfected the subtle violence of swallowing my rage and shame, then let it rain down on myself. He was never that clever.

Part of not being him is that in outliving him (he died at age 38) I have claimed a natural victory, a landmark that I did my best to make sure I'd never achieve, as if the act of outliving him was forbidden to me.

I could go on and on about years of bulimia, of vomiting 30 times a day; I could write forever of the simple and very complicated act of self-annihilation. I could tell you about what it was like to destroy myself day after day for decades. I could write an encyclopedia on self-abuse, I could take you on a very private river boat trip down the clogged toilet of my own vomit and shame; give you a free pass into the desert of emotional starvation. I could, but I won't. You wouldn't understand, and besides, I no longer wish to explain. I don't have to. I don't pity myself, I don't mourn the wasting of part of my life. I understand anger and I understand violence in all its symphonic cacophony and I understand terrible pride and that I will not lie on my deathbed like Tolstoy's Ivan Ilych and seek and be granted grace and enlightenment by revealing myself, by humbling myself.

It's not that interesting to me anymore, largely because I managed to live despite my best efforts to the contrary. The years of attempted self-murder have taken their toll on me in terms of ingrained dysfunction. I have had no recovery, no great breakthrough; I had all the insights my world would allow, and none of the motivation to act on them. I merely outlasted myself.

In some circles, this might pass as a triumph. Not to me. I simply set out finish what my father started, ultimately failed, but found my reflection in the explosion of rage in a porcelain universe.

My humiliation, my frustration here on

St. Maarten is a daily event. I'm living in a place where I'm alone in the prison of my own language, imbuing others in print with qualities they're too lazy to find for themselves, let alone see in me. Here I am, your humble psychological servant at work. Each day I come back for a methodical beating. You can take the boy out of the bathhouse, but you can't take the bathhouse out of the boy.

Forget the stupid earlier salmon imagery, not to mention the journey into Freudian sentimentality. More and more I feel like one of those dinosaurs that got trapped in the La Brea tar pits and died because it couldn't extricate itself from its sticky prison of memory. Or maybe, I'm serving my time here in the name of karma; I have some lesson to learn about the continued merits of relentless self-abuse and I'm stuck here in my fucked-up humiliation and shame until I figure my sick soul's way out.

A Dominicano Primer to Panicky Auto-eroticism Reprinted from the St. Maarten Guardian, May 6, 1998

Congratulations.

Your decision to visit the Dominican Republic is a good one. It is a beautiful place. A place of history and mystery; a magical place that leaps out at you like a Fauvist painting, all wild and vibrant colors that almost seem to shimmy and dance.

And why not? This is a country that has its own sound track, music on every corner, in every room, the slightly nutty and hysterical guitar strains of Bachata hanging in the air.

So, like I said, you've made a good choice. Despite its very real and devastating pockets of poverty, squalor and unemployment, the Dominican Republic is an honest to goodness country, independent and real; poetic and unexpected, it defies preconceptions. For better or worse, mainly worse, this is the country of Christopher Columbus and colonialism. But it's a place that holds a weirdly benign view of its colonial past, perhaps it is even proud of it, though the gradations of this beneficence are likely dependent on the lighter shade of skin color and economic status of the Dominicano in question.

But if there is one thing you must know about the Dominican Republic, beyond its vast beauty, its birds and flowers, beyond the fact that its soil is as rich with peleteros (baseball players) as it is with produce and provision, it is that it is home to perhaps the worst drivers in the Caribbean.

I was going to say worst in the world, but a certain St. Maarten-based Nigerian newspaper editor said that the drivers in his homeland claim that title hands down. Others have nominated the anarchic Italians, the Egyptians, the denizens of one Venezuelan city who put the "c-a-r" in Caracas, and the motorists of any city in India.

So the Dominicano drivers will have to settle for worst in the Caribbean. Not malicious, mind you, just bad. There is an historical precedent. Christopher Columbus basically found the place by accident, just ran into it, and local drivers ever since have been operating much the same way.

You think French Quarter drivers are bad on St. Martin? You ain't seen nothing yet. For more reading on the subject, I refer you to Jesus van Enkvort-Cedeno's seminal yet highly fictional treatise, "Auto-eroticism In Post-Colonial Societies. A primer."

Some things to consider when driving in Santo Domingo and La Republica: — throw out the rule book and expect anything. Cars, trucks, buses coming at you from all angles, including head on, at all speeds. Ubiquitous motor bikes that swarm around like some alien battalion of huge, motorized insects, always humming, always buzzing, always annoying.

These motorbikes and their drivers accomplish some very remarkable feats. It's not unusual to see extra-large gas tanks, boxes containing TVs and microwave ovens, and some two or three passengers, each of them carrying something, perched on one of these things. I saw one guy on a motorbike in Santiago driving with a small refrigerator placed on his lap, all but blocking his line of vision. It didn't seem to faze him.

Here's a fashion tip. For you ladies who will be visiting the Dominican Republic who favor skirts, take note of the way that female passengers in la Republica sit side-saddle on the bikes.

The Dominican Republic has very good main roads. All the better for very large trucks, buses, cars, motor bikes and the occasional horse or mule to make long distance trips. The speed limit is however fast you want to go, horses included. The sound barrier is broken daily on these roads, but nobody ever notices because it's too loud.

Beware of slow moving trucks carrying a ton of plantains that travel in the left lane, and huge construction trucks going at 135 kilometers per hour in the right lane, or between two lanes, or on the shoulder of the road.

Remember, motorists cut directly across the highway at any time, so any unfenced, non-barricaded point is an exit or entry to either the highway, a roadside village, or oblivion.

Also, cars and trucks pass on the right, stop in the middle of the highway without signaling, and emit diesel fumes worthy of the best bronchial-pulmonary abominations this side of Mexico City.

In short, driving in the D.R. is not just a way of getting around, it is a near-death experience producing the same type of physical effects that might be achieved drinking six strong espressos during the course of a panic attack.

All in all, exhilarating. So good luck, keep calm, update that insurance, and remember, it could be worse; it could be Lagos.

**You can lead a St. Maartener to culture, but you can't make him, or her, think...
One Sunday, 1997**

Cultural forum today on the radio. The usual suspects, Sekou, Louie Laveist, Clara Reyes, Debbie Jack, somebody from the French side, talking the nationalist talk in "round table" format moderated by Badejo. They discuss things like vanishing indigenous culture, what is St. Maarten's cultural paradigm, no one knows, the significance of living in a polyglot culture and so on, though no one broaches the mediocrity issue and the lack of critical structure. It's a bit self-congratulatory, but it's not bad, and Badejo is doing an intelligent job keeping the discussion in focus.

Then things deteriorate when Clara says she speaks that African language that is communicated by clicks and she starts clicking away, click and clack. Kung, I think it's called. Then they all congratulate her for clicking even though no one knows what she's said or if in fact it's authentic at all.

Soon it all reverts to the usual platitudes of the uniqueness of St. Maarten culture and the self-assuring reminders that the rest of the Caribbean is just waiting to hear, dance to, read or just plain fuck whatever next comes out of here.

I like Fabian and always have. I just wish he would drop his nice guy persona and come down on them a bit, challenge them, but he doesn't because he has, at this point in his life, convinced himself that he is one of them, and their achievements ennoble him and justify his role among them. It's not that simple for me.

At times like this, I miss the smartass smack of American radio, especially Jim Rome, host of the "Jungle" program in L.A. I'm wondering what the man in the box, Romey, might say about all this. Probably something like, "St. Maarten nationalists, your stuff is just so tired. Stop marrying your cousins, stop patting yourself on the back, and stop clicking. Good night now. "
I "click" off the radio leaving Louie Laveist dangling in thin dead air.

September 1998

I'm sitting at my desk on the usual Sunday afternoon shift when who walks in but "Dr." Jack Stevens. This in itself is not unique. Each Sunday he either faxes or brings in personally his little contribution to the Guardian called "Prescription for Success." I won't abuse my keyboard by describing it to you in depth, so let's just say it's as lame as lame can be.

Most days, Happy Jack is as sunny and chatty as a glass of ice tea laced with the amphetamine of your choice, but today, he kind of skulks in like a sheep with a hangover and it doesn't take me long to figure it out. The 50ish conservative Mr. Middle America Missionary motherfucker has gone and shaved his head and his white beard as well. All this eerie absence of his normal hair makes him seem whiter than ever despite the fact he's got a tomato colored kind of sunburn. His skull and cheeks glow like they're radio active. I wonder if he and the misses, Asha Stevens, got busy the night before and decided to give each other "haircuts" and then something went a little sado-masochistically wrong. He hands me the "prescription for success" which has something to do with the six features of a born leader and I sit there open mouthed and blinded by whiteness until he turns and leaves.

Summer and fall Fridays 1998

Since the Guardian does not publish on Saturday and there is no deadline to meet, Friday is generally a kind of relaxing day. I've spent many, many Friday afternoons with Mosera at his gallery or at his house just discussing this and that, opining away. One of many interesting things about Mosera is that he keeps me off-balance in the way he can change gears and leapfrog subjects. He's got a real jazzy mind, and that's probably one of the reasons we got to know each other; he's never boring. His gallery is something of a sanctuary for me, my chance to get off the Philipsburg streets and out of the circus my life has become.

One Friday he's telling me, "you know what I don't like? I don't like it when some man comes in and tells you, 'I'm the kind of guy who won't take no for an answer.' If he's got to tell you what kind of guy he is, than he's probably not what he thinks. He's just pusillanimous."

Then, not missing a beat, he turns to me and asks me, "what kind of guy are you?"

I'm the kind of guy who doesn't answer those kinds of questions. I'm an ironic Byronic hero. But, if you push me for a definition, I'm the kind of guy who can't take yes for an answer. I'm the kind of guy who would commit the perfect crime and then solve it.

Mosera ignores my ignoring of his question and waits a minute or two and begins to talk about art and Axum, the empire he wants to create, the paintings he loves and cannot sell, the CD he wants to record, fresh oranges and the importance of Aries creatures like the two of us to tramp the ground in front of us. A couple of more hours pass by and Mosera looks at me. "Are you hiding from somebody," he asks.

If he only knew.

Going on the Offensive
Reprinted from the St. Maarten Guardian, April 17, 1998

Who says there's no limit to offensive ideas?

Not me, especially now I've seen that the Reggae Cafe is up and running, unabashedly trying to make some quick bucks on the brilliant legacy of Bob Marley, the commercial appeal of Reggae, and by displaying stereotypical images of Rastafarians and related subject matter on goods for sale in a less than flattering fashion.

The premise of the Reggae Cafe has far less to do with the concepts of "giving Jah thanks and praises," than it does with selling "Buffalo Soldier wings" and "jahbasco" sauce, all in the apparent general pursuit of money, money, money. After all, Jah provide the bread.

Since I got in touch with my offensive side, this kind of thing doesn't bother me anymore. Really. Call me assimilated, but I've learned to embrace the gauche. So here's a recipe for offensive cultural entrepreneurship I'd like to share with you.

Take a group of business types, expose them to an indigenous, roots culture that has produced an unparalleled body of musical work and certifiable icons, and then attempt to cash in.

Take it, exploit it, cheapen it, all in good fun, of course. Then, a Reggae Cafe logo on a T-shirt, offer up "I shot the Sheriff" shots and count the money. "Dem belly full, but we hungry..."

Let em' eat cake, at least for now, because I have exciting "offensive" news to share with you. Next month, St. Maarten will play host to a Gospel Festival. Let's see. Gospel, like Reggae is popular. Gospel, like Reggae is roots music. Gospel, like Reggae can be exploited. Boo-yah. I'm seizing the moment. I'm going to open the Gospel Cafe. I know it's not original. I'm just following in the footsteps of the purveyors of the Reggae Cafe. I see it as an offensive merger of the already commercialized Hard Rock Cafe, and that untapped gold mine which is Gospel.

Praise the lord, and pass the profits. And not necessarily in that order.

We'll offer Shirley Caesar salad, and Hallelujah hot dogs with messiah mustard. And lest I forget, our menu topper is the M.C. Hammer-burger. Can't touch this.

Offensive enough? Offensive like "Roots beef in jahbasco sauce?" Let me continue.

Don't forget our drink specials. The "Resurrection" will make you feel like you are floating, like you can save humanity.

Don't forget our line of stupid, unoriginal T-shirts, caps, and visors. Offensive enough?

I plan an offensive empire. Coming soon, the Koran Cafe, complete with Jihad jerky. It's delicious. How about the Kosher Cafe? Try our beef tips in Jewbasco sauce. Bad taste, or does it just taste bad?

How about Hinduville? Our slogan is, "we curry your favor." And finally, the jewel in my offensive crown, the Satan Cafe. Try the damnation deluxe platter; it's hot as hell. The only thing that can stop me, even as I type away in my offensive private cell, is people actually showing good taste and turning away from the mindless, heartless exploitation and co-opting of images they have no claim to, and that are not for sale. It could happen.

But I'm counting on being wrong about this, or else my empire of the offensive is in peril. And, just like the Reggae Cafe, I'm going to be stuck with a lot of offensive merchandise. Not to mention a significant Karmic burden.

December 1998

Satan, tell Andy what he's won...

Big discussion in the Guardian today among me, Georgina, Germina, Esther, Francisco and Symmea concerning how many of the Ten Commandments each of us has broken. Typically, the women come in on the low side, maybe admitting to five or six commandment breaks at the most.

On instinct, I think Symmea might be

holding back a few, but we're on the honor system here, so I let her go.

Francisco says he's not sure exactly how many he's broken, but he's a man, and he's a French Caribbean man at that, so I estimate he has seven, at least, probably could pencil him in for eight. As for me, I think I can honestly admit to nine, so I win this little Guardian game show, or make that, I lose.
Hey Satan, tell Andy what's in store now that its official he's a liar, adulterer, thief and all-around commandment breaker.

How about a one way ticket to damnation with a complimentary set of asbestos luggage. And there's more. A nice private room in hell next door to my father with live and taped coverage of Island Council meetings piped in 24 hours a day for eternity.
At least I still have "thou shall not kill" on my plus side, though you never know what might happen if I don't get out of here soon.

Fast Eddy
Summer, 1994

Besides criticizing St. Maarten, one other way I stay sharp is by running. Every morning I take off from the small house in the

Lowlands and run up and down hills toward the sea. One morning this crazy looking, muscular tan colored dog comes running at me full speed, his tongue hanging out, his jaw jutting forward in true St. Maarten style, shiny brown eyes with no one home. Shit, I'm thinking this dog is either rabid or on drugs, and I start yelling at him and making motions for him to go away. But it does no good, and soon the dog is all over my lower leg, licking my calf, and rubbing his head against my knee.

Three Haitian guys sitting by the dumpster waiting for a ride to work find this whole scene unimaginably funny. I've never heard anyone laugh so loud, especially in Creole, as these guys. Pretty strange, but maybe not that strange when you consider that Haitians enjoy a nice roasted cat every now and then.

By now, I realize this dog has attached himself to me and will follow me till he drops. We run side by side for a couple of miles, him making this chukah, chukah sound as he trots. About 30 minutes later I meet my wife at the beach where she is waiting with our "other" dog, Ackee.

She sees the tan dog jogging beside me and comments on how good looking he is, not me, and how he's obviously been cared for and well treated. Meanwhile, I'm washing three gallons of his slobber off of my left leg.

We don't know quite what do with him as I hop in the car and ride back up the hill with my wife. I look behind, and in the best tradition of sentimental lost dog movies, there's the beast running up the hill following the car as if we tied a pork chop to the back, playing the pitiful drama for all he's worth.

Finally, we give in, open the door and the dog pops into the backseat next to Ackee who barely blinks at his arrival, as if it's some canine conspiracy meant to exploit the soft-headed and soft-hearted among us.

I feed the dog and give him some water and he promptly falls asleep on the porch, looking for all the world like he's lived here all his life. I decide to call him Eddy, because he looks like an Eddy, Fast Eddy, and besides, I was listening to Electric Avenue by Eddy Grant on my Walkman when the beast adopted me.

The boys in Grand Case

Black birds vaulting
to an orange orb
endangered species
suspended like commas
floating-
the elegant drama
of an elbow to the chest
discreet and sweet
the sweaty joy of seeing the universe
drop into a hoop
pure,
like black birds who have not
learned how to fall
not yet seen the ground rushing up
to greet them like a mad butler
shining the bottom of their feet, whispering
basketball
makes angels of us all

"Whom the god's would destroy they first deprive of his magic" Rafi Zabor

I remember the exact day I died. Not literally, but rather when the magic of my childhood died, my innocence left me forever.

It was a Sunday in August 1965. I was seven years old and had been spending the summer with my family at a bungalow colony in Rockland County, New York. My mother and father were divorced by now, and I had been seeing him regularly over the summer on Sunday visitations.

Apparently, he was acting so scary, that my younger sister did not want to go on these visits, but visitation laws being what they were, one of us had to go, and I, as the elder was the one. Each Sunday became successively more frightening and tense for me, wondering not when I was going to be beaten, but how, and what I could possibly have done to warrant such rage being visited upon me.

One afternoon, after being returned home following a particularly soul-killing day of abuse and terror, I found myself walking around, being conscious of my steps, fearing I was being followed, watching my shadow for signs of betrayal.

Not far from where I was walking was the small bungalow rented by Paddy and Lina. He was retired, and his main hobby was to go fishing for carp and pike at the big reservoir a few miles down the road. On this day, he had either been too good a fisherman or had found too few takers for his fish, because I saw about four or five of them, cast aside, laying on melting ice, waiting to die.

I picked up a stick and began to torture the fish, poking their eyes out, killing them with a controlled and curious rage. I don't know how long I was there, but Lina caught sight of me and yelled at me to stop, and so I dropped the stick and ran and ran and ran. I have not stopped running since that day.

I know very well why I did what I did and that it was in reaction to my father's beating of me and my helpless seven-year-old rage. I've done a lot of shitty things in my life. I've hurt people and I've hurt myself. But torturing the fish was the single worst thing I've ever done.

You see, someone killed my soul early on, and no one said a word, least of all me. That's sad, and I think it's a terrible thing to witness the desecration of your innocent magic. But it's even worse to participate in your own doom by torturing creatures more helpless than you as they sit already dying in fading sunlight.

Oh Carolina
Autumn, 1994

No justice for the Mullet Bay four who were convicted and sentenced in the murder of a Dutch banker, even though no weapon or other hard evidence was found. It was kind of like round up the usual crack addicted suspects from Dominica and Anguilla and let's get it over with.

Justice in the Antillean court system is a joke to begin with. Sweaty white Dutch judges speaking stilted English passing judgment on a population that is easily 90 percent non-white and of a completely different culture.

The justice system contains no provision for bail, or for adequate representation. The native language for the judges, prosecutors and many of the lawyers is Dutch, for those charged, it is either English or Spanish, with Dutch, French, and patois, or Creole third. To add insult to injury in this case, the public defender for two of the Mullet Bay four, a St. Maarten lawyer named Maxime Larmonie didn't even try to fake giving his clients a good defense. He was bored, unprepared and out of it.

Next day, the Guardian gets a letter from

Caroline Peterson of Simpson Bay. Ms. Peterson writes that what went on in the court room shocked her. She calls Larmonie inept and questions whether he should be allowed to practice law.

Two prominent Antilleans, one a noted notary, are standing in the entrance way to the Guardian, discussing the letter. One says that "it's good to have someone in the profession commenting on this." The other thinks he might have even dated Caroline at one time and knows her from Aruba.

Actually, "Caroline Peterson" is my wife, Jenny Li, and as far as I know, she's never been to law school, let alone Aruba.

Forget ("National") Press Day
Reprinted from the St. Maarten Guardian, September 1, 1998

Normally, I adhere to the philosophy of Groucho Marx who once said, "I wouldn't want to belong to any group that would have me for a member."

Fortunately, or unfortunately, I don't have to worry when the organization in question is the dormant St. Maarten Press Association. Today is National Press Day and we, the St. Maarten media, are apparently doing nothing to commemorate it.

Why? Who knows? But it's unfortunate that we have not made an effort to come together because this has been a tough year for the media.

First, on the eve of Press Day last year, there was the order by the Telecommunication Bureau banning Radio Curom and Radio Tropical from broadcasting at certain hours. A judicial order saved the day, but the tone was set for an edgy year. Next came the order to have a several second tape delay on live radio call-in shows. This was spurred on by the alleged use of profanity on certain shows in Curaçao.

Then we had former Minister Martha Dijkhoff visiting St. Maarten to talk about a "National Media Policy" including just who should own media houses.

Interspersed with all this was the Executive Council pulling the plug on the weekly, live GIS press briefings because they could not sufficiently control what was going on and found certain questions not to be to their liking.

A few months ago, then president of parliament-elect, Errol Cova, told the media he basically expected their cooperation.

Much more recently, voices and questions were raised when it was reported that one individual had designs on a newspaper and radio station and that the certain individual in question might begin an attempt to monopolize the media.

A constant side dish to this media buffet of discontent are the selective and on-going feuds among politicians and media members concerning allegations of bias, manipulation, misinformation and ostracism.

Given everything that has happened in this past journalistic calendar year, and in years past, why isn't the St. Maarten media organized and unionized?

At first glance, it might appear that this is due to a certain type of lethargy and apathy; we are too busy scraping around for news and simply do not care enough to organize, stay focused and operate as a valid media union. We are fractionalized by the type of media house we represent, nationality, political ideology, rivalries and personality conflicts.

But I think the subtext to our lack of becoming a serious entity is the nature of the job we do, and where we do it. Our reporting is very much of the "he said, she said," type, often lacking balance and bite because almost every issue, every news item, is politically generated and motivated, and is geared, weighted and packaged for its maximum partisan usage.

In a political system that allows no structure for dynamic democratic change, where issues are discussed in endlessly repetitive terms without any real resolution, we, as a media, I think, become suppressed and sedated by the dull repetition of what we have to report and the fact that it happens in such a vacuum.

After a while, as the same news stories recycle and the line between political parties, newsworthiness and reality becomes increasingly blurred, one can ask the question, is there any point in what I'm doing, when nothing really changes?

A journalist's ostensible job is to keep the public informed and to perform this service accurately and in an unbiased manner. This is a very daunting task in St. Maarten given the partisan posturing and spin control that whirl around every spoken and written word. I'd say balance is more of a problem than bias.

One might argue that all the media houses, to some extent, fulfill their job descriptions in terms of providing information, especially of the political variety and covering events, if not meaningful issues.

As a group, we are neither aggressive nor critical enough. We condone and in some cases cultivate mediocrity, rather than raising the quality bar higher and higher.

We have not taken a stand to establish our rights to access public information. It baffles me that, in this age of "open government," we still have no access to records and documents and that we have made no noise as a group about opening up such documents under a Freedom of Information Act.

Basically, in terms of the Island Government, we are on a need to know basis. That's not enough. We are a free press, but not quite. Uncensored, but self-limiting. Think about the inherent wisdom in *Concrete Jungle* when Bob Marley sings, "no chains around my feet, but I'm not free."

Forget Press Day, especially National Press Day. The situation here on St. Maarten is unique; we are the heirs to the legacy of Joe Lake Sr., the man who founded the Windward Islands Opinion.

In his memory, we should take a look at how we are doing our jobs; why we keep the cycle of partisan non-news alive, and what all of it might say about how we function as journalists, and whether we might need to reconsider if that is in fact a correct fable.

In the end, all any of us who type for a living and hunt down semi-truths really have is our integrity; that we cannot be bought or sold, and that in the spirit of Joe Lake Sr., we are not afraid to bite the hand that tries to feed us lies.

Saba, your goats rock
New Year's 1996

My wife Jenny Li and I went to Saba for New Year's eve thinking it would be a quiet escape from St. Martin, where any occasion is marked by setting off enough fireworks to put NATO forces on alert.

We thought Saba would be quiet. We were wrong. Saba is a ten minute flight from St. Maarten, but it's not for the faint hearted. The plane comes in snugly beside the mountainous edge of the island, slips down in a drastically vertical resolution and somehow manages to stop on a short runway whose terminus is the Caribbean Sea.

Watching planes land is one of the big activities for Sabans.

Saba is a tiny, dormant volcano of a mountainous island that literally climbs out of the sea and keeps rising. Its five square miles house about 1,500 goats, 1,200 people, half black, half white and all kind of flaky, made even more so by living on this bizarre little island that looks like a Swiss village dropped into the sparkling Caribbean.

The main families on Saba are the Hassels and the Johnsons. Most everyone is related and looks eerily the same, especially the whites, who are fair-haired and virtually chinless.

Anyway, just before midnight, the fireworks and noisemakers begin. We can hear them from the hotel we're staying at which has a panoramic view of the island. Comes midnight, and more noise. Comes one a.m. and those hard partying Sabans are still at it, laughing and singing and dancing with their goats and chickens.

By two a.m., I've decided I'm going to find the closest Hassell and kill him, and then start working my way through the Johnsons, Linzeys, Sortons, Heyligers and right on down the list. By three a.m. it's over, and I fall asleep with beer-drinking goats and saucy Sabans making merry around me, while believe it or not, I cannot wait to get back to nice, quiet Colombier.

"To set up what you like against what you dislike—this is the disease of the mind."
Seng-T'San

August 1998

Someday I'll achieve something; something worth achieving. Not recognition or money, but something more like the apotheosis of self-expression. My own voice won't sound foolish or forced to me. Something perfect, like Aretha Franklin singing "Angel", or Marvin Gaye singing "Lets Get it On", or TS Eliot's poetic voice in "The Love Song of J. Alfred Prufrock", or Van Gogh's brush strokes in "Crows Over a Wheat Field". Something Gerard Manley Hopkins perfect. Something, anything. Until then, I act and write the fool in the Guardian, doing my best (there, an admission) and having no one even notice it; pushing the parameters of what can and cannot be done in journalism here and being ignored.

I'm just someone in the wrong place at the wrong time seeking recognition for something I cannot even own in the first place. Does this make sense? I guess not. I wish I could sing, because then my voice could tell you the story of my longing, but I can't sing.

When I sing, dogs commit suicide.

It's impossible to say what I feel.

I'm an asshole to be writing this; a fool, letting you see my passion added, divided, trapped like the beads on some human abacus.

That Question Mark Remains
Reprinted from the St. Maarten Guardian, September 3, 1997

The sun goes up and the sun goes down and each day passes; you take it for granted, much like the faces you see every day, until one day you don't see them anymore. Globally, the first example that leaps to mind is the late Princess Diana. But locally, there is another story, and though the subject is not famous, hers was also a life that had equal parts of tragedy, pathos, grace and charity.

Cynthia Lorraine Walters died September 1. She was three months past her 50th birthday, and one gets the impression many of those adult years— some spent on the streets, some in the care of others, were not easy.

I first encountered Walters about three years ago. She would walk up and down the street; her mind wrapped in that type of co-

coon of mental illness of those who have seemingly been hurt in a way beyond repair, their gears of reality stripped and left hanging.

At night, she would sleep in front of the Post Office, a slight woman, her body curled in the shape of a question mark.

No one is exactly sure what happened to shape Walter's life. But what is more certain is that Walters had a number of people in the community who watched out for her. Actually, they did a lot more than that.

Some like Dr. Alma K. Rogers-Fleming took her into their homes for months at a time, clothed her, fed her, loved her. Others like Women's Aglow St. Maarten, and her last caretakers Adelia Brazoa and Cassilda van der Neut, seemed to be on the lookout for her spiritual needs as well.

"Only God knows what happened to her," said Brazoa, "but in the last year of her life, she was fed and loved."

Brazoa said Walters was first hospitalized at the St. Maarten Medical Center (SMMC) because of problems with an ulcer. She was hospitalized for more than a month. Dr. Maurice Ferrier of the SMMC said it was hospital practice not to reveal the cause of death, saying that information had to come from the family of the deceased.

Brazoa said only, "when a person lives on the street so long, their body is not taken care of, things happen."

Rogers-Fleming, who was visibly upset about Walters death and the long illness and hospitalization that preceded it, said she thought Walters' time in Suriname at a religious retreat sponsored by Brazoa and friends worsened her condition.

"She didn't even remember my name," Rogers-Fleming said sadly, recalling that she gave Walters her daughter's room, and that Walters cooked dinner on Saturdays.

"She had been shunned for so long, she was so outside of things, she felt like a reject," Rogers-Fleming said of Walters' more extended lucid and socially integrated times when she actually had a chance at a life.

What now seems like a very long time ago, I asked former Commissioner and head of social welfare affairs Mrs. Elaine Gumbs-Vlaun about Walters and homelessness on St. Maarten. Gumbs-Vlaun acknowledged in 1994 it was a growing problem, and one that would likely get worse as the network of extended families died out, or the type of "difficult homeless", i.e. drug abusers or violent persons, increased.

Three years later, there is still no homeless shelter, no place for those who have fallen between the cracks to seek safer refuge if they are bereft of church, friends and family.

The sun rises and the sun sets and you can look over to the Post Office, and observe Max Pandt picking up his mail, this one and that one coming and going. Walters is no longer there, but that question mark, that shape that was her life, remains.

Recently

There was a story in the Herald that local Judge Bob Witt had ruled that chronic Pointe Blanche Prison inmate and generally insane man Allen Richardson write for the Herald. Richardson is a prolific letter writer and equally prolific consumer of crack.

Reportedly, Richardson almost passed out when he learned of his extraordinary sentence.

I cannot figure out if this is added punishment for Richardson or for the people of St. Maarten who will be subjected to his lunatic, crack-fueled flights of keyboard excrement. I have to admit that if I were a prisoner and made to work at the Herald, I'd immediately call it cruel and unusual punishment and a fate worse than death. I'd appeal and appeal, I'd sell a kidney and hire Johnnie Cochran.

In fact, I'd rather wash the toilets at the prison with a toothbrush, my own, than hang out with the stilted colonialists at the Herald. Tough luck Allen, knock 'em dead.

Bytes and Bites
Reprinted from the St. Maarten Guardian, January 15, 1999

Bytes and bites, bits and blurbs from the curb.

Unruly rumblings.

Let's be Frank. On second hand, let's be glad we're not. You have to feel sorry for Frank Mingo, the minister of finance who is a nice man.

He has been taking all kinds of blows from all kinds of people. Will he or won't he survive the Machiavellian actions going on behind the scenes?

Whatever happens, Frank had to have known somewhere down deep that he was in for trouble. Remember, taking on the job of finance minister in this wretched economy as he did several months ago, was tantamount to accepting the position of the captain of the Titanic after being told it was going to sink.

Still, you have to feel for him, however self-inflicted his wounds might be. He is a decent guy who wanted to bring a private sector mentality to the endless red tape of Curaçao's island government and civil service paralysis. According to several politicians, including Sen. Clyde van Putten, he's being set up to take the fall for an incompetent, bankrupt and visionless government.

Look at the bright side. If he loses at ministerial Bingo, Mingo can always get into journalism and start the Red (DP) News. Don't laugh, everybody is doing it.

Dave Levenstone has a paper in Saba. The St. Maarten Hospitality and Trades Association has a newspaper, Endangered Antilleans have one — The Champion.

KABNA has its newspaper, hint, it's called The Daily Herald, and there was the St. Maarten Love Punch for awhile, until it ran out of gas.

Anything is possible. Buzz and the Bull Dog may one day be publishing a National Enquirer style paper that accurately reflects both the tenor and quality of their radio show, as well as the society around them, i.e. Glenn Carty, man of the year, at least according to two newspapers.

If that's not enough, get this. It appears that the Big Blue, the St. Maarten Patriotic Alliance (SPA), is gearing up to put out its own newspaper. The word is they want to get the publication out as soon as possible in order to blitzkrieg the voting public with their warm and fuzzy messages of empowerment and news of their successes over the past 16 months. Good luck. I'm looking forward to the balanced reporting, unbiased coverage and stimulating copy.

Under questions to be asked and answered, whatever happened to "Pan Man" the first feature movie based on a play by Ian Valz to be shot in St. Maarten? What kind of party will Vance James join or form? Has Julian Rollocks used up his nine political lives? Is St. Maarten's social and intellectual growth unduly impaired by the religious right fundamentalist element in the community?

Shouldn't St. Maarten liberalize its laws on marijuana? After all, if it's legal in certain sections of Holland, by extension, shouldn't the same standards apply here given that St. Maarten is a colony of the Netherlands? It's a great cash crop and it is far less harmful than alcohol or tobacco, both of which are "legal" drugs.

And speaking of possible illegalities, what about Caribe Waste Technology Inc.? Did they implode, explode or disappear until after the results of the Island council elections? One last thing, a quick note to herbalist John Edwards who said in an irresponsible newspaper article last week in The Daily Herald that he can cure people with AIDS. Share the secret, win a Nobel Prize, really save some lives.

Otherwise, you're just a fraud trying to make money off of ailing people desperate to be healed.

Mack daddy
August, 1997

"Sweet" Leroy Richardson, well known felon, promoter and über St. Maartener, can now add the title of pimp to his long resume. Sweet Leroy, accompanied by a fat, late 40ish Dutch guy in short pants sweating beer, informs me he is opening an "escort" service. Call girls, I mean escorts, are being imported to St. Maarten for the purpose of getting this going. Sweet Leroy is coy when it comes to how much it will cost to be escorted, but says the fee will be high enough to make this a "classy operation."

The Dutch guy doesn't say much, but it's obvious he's the money behind Leroy. Leroy is the local St. Maartener fronting for the business license. They want this written up in the newspaper like it's a viable new business. Prostitution is not legal in St. Maarten, but it is permitted and pervasive. There are several whore houses including the aptly named "Seaman's Club" and Carmen Priest's place, where some nights there are so many cars parked by the building it looks like Carmen and her staff are giving it away for free.

I ask Leroy if the call girls, I mean, escorts, are expected to have sex with the customers. Leroy says what goes on between the two adults is their own business, but admits that the course of a night's events might lead to intercourse, of course. Only he doesn't use the word intercourse.

The fat Dutch guy says he wants to read the newspaper "write up" before it goes in the paper. With any normal story I'd say no, the

Guardian reserves editorial privilege. But this is extremely not normal. It's the equivalent of pimping for a pimp, which is pimp squared. I just say nothing, knowing full well I'll never type a word about it for print, though our competition, The Herald, certainly will.

My young colleague Wendie Brown, who's been listening in, asks Sweet Leroy if male escorts will be available for women. Of course, he says.

Then Wendie asks if the male escorts would be available to men as well as women.

Leroy is genuinely shocked, though just a few years earlier he earned considerable notoriety for promoting a show that featured female impersonators. "This is about regular pussy," he tells Wendie, as if he's lecturing her on table etiquette.

"This is classy. Nobody said anything about faggots."

PJIA Towing Blues
Reprinted from the St. Maarten Guardian, January 12, 1999

There was a man Friday at Princess Juliana International Airport (PJIA) cursing a blue streak up one side of the facility and down the other. He was cursing objects, individuals and his fate

This wasn't crazy, incoherent cursing. No, this was cause and effect cursing. This was a meteor shower of expletives delivered like a dance hall DJ in a very ugly mood, you know, like in the comic books. *4@#kl&&@!*, a veritable pearl necklace of profane gems strung together with true venom.

It was a tour de force of profanity. A profane refrain.

Naturally, when somebody is going off like that you don't stick your head in there and say "excuse me sir, what has you so upset? And, by the way, I'm also so glad you're unarmed."

It didn't take me long to figure out what made the man apoplectic. It seems his car was towed. He'd left it in the "unload zone" a little too long and the eager beaver security guards and towers put their collective obstinance and unreasonableness together and towed his vehicle. Never mind about making a public announcement first alerting the specific motorist and identifying the vehicle by license plate number, thus giving him or her a fair chance. Nope. The man was mumbling about"Babylon" and combining wild expletives in very creative combinations as he received his receipt. You see, it costs

$75 to get one's towed vehicle back. And on this day, the airport was not particularly busy, there was a minimal number of taxis and car drop-offs in the area.

Which brings me to the subject of tow-truck empathy. Right after the cursing man departed and began the process of getting his car back, I noticed that my car, which had been left in the unload zone for all of three minutes while I paid my departure tax of $20, which is a rip-off story of a different kind, was next.

Anyway, to advance this annoying story to its inevitable expensive and irritating conclusion, I arrived back at my car to see it being freshly loaded on to the tow. I mean the process had literally just begun when I arrived.

If the security guard had shown the slightest bit of common sense, flexibility and/or kindness, the car could have been released just as I arrived, but expecting common sense, kindness or flexibility is like expecting water from the moon. It doesn't happen, especially at PJIA.

I decided to go gangster. I took a $100 bill out of my wallet and waved it in the face of the car tower. "Let the car go and take the money. Show some heart and buck the system." For a split second, he might have been tempted.But the flicker in his eyes passed. So, there went the car. And then, like some Magic Mind came down and passed a wand over me, I turned into "Cursing Man" myself. A M4@$———F*&$@#———, here, an A———, there. I amazed myself with my adrenalized tour of the very bottom of the bowels of the linguistic food chain.

I'm not proud of it. Mainly because it didn't work.

Now, are there spelled out rules for exactly how long one can park in "no-park" unload zone? How many cars are towed per week; do they tow more often when it is less busy to generate more money? And, is one company doing all the towing or are the spoils being spread around. Also, how much money does PJIA make off of all these tows and what are they using it for? I called the security and the accounting departments at PJIA and came up with nothing save that all information and public comments would have to come from PJIA managing director Eugene Holiday. Bad odds on that. I have a better chance of becoming Pope than hearing from Holiday.

Anyway, it cost me $95 to leave St. Maarten Friday: $75 for the tow and $20 for the extortion, er, I mean departure tax.

My cursing precursor was absolutely right—the PJIA revenue generating engine is every inch Babylon.

Oasis

I was walking among the ruins
imagining Moses and sand dunes
when I came upon two typewriters sitting on opposite walls
of what was once a beautiful temple
stalks of green weeds remind you,
what is the basis for this oasis?
Two typewriters sitting like stalled prophets
I thought I'd sit down and write you a letter
all the better to hand it to you
from such a holy place
but the keys were rusted and stuck
unemotional and mechanical
just another exquisite writer's block
stalks of green weeds remind me of you
what is the basis for this oasis
I'm not one to linger, I left the keys for dead
just machines I said,
but dread flooded my locks
my fingers were useless
and I saw your face in such a holy place
amid stalks of green weeds

they remind me of you
what is the basis for this oasis?

August 1998
Meh a-tell ya, meh jes wanna big up da youts

Jamaican dancehall artists Goofy and Red Rat are on St. Maarten today promoting their concert tonight. I saw Red Rat eating a huge plate of food at the Jerk Restaurant. The name of the restaurant has nothing to do with the personalities of Archie and Anita who run it. They're nice, not jerks. Jerk is a style of Jamaican cooking. After eating, Red Rat and Goofy appeared on Lloyd Richardson's popular afternoon radio program on PJD2.

What happened next truly defies description because I'm not sure anyone can say exactly what was said on air. Both Red Rat and Goofy have real thick Jamaican accents and speak mainly Jamaican patois. So Lloyd would ask a question and Red Rat would begin, "meh tell yah" and then not speak a readily recognizable English word for about five minutes when he would surface out of the thick patois and continue, "it's all about biggin' up da youts" and on and on it went.

The same thing for Goofy. Lloyd asks him

something and he begins a fifteen minute discourse, none of which anyone in the studio understands until he finally says, "yah know mon, it's all about the love. Givin' and takin' it. Goofy always want to big up da love."

Because Lloyd cannot figure out what's being said, he doesn't interrupt either artist with questions. It is, unintentionally, the funniest 25 minutes of radio Lloyd has ever done.

December 1999

Five years after I first set foot here, just thinking about St. Maarten still makes me angry. I thought writing about it might help, but the words have led to no transformation. Why the anger? Maybe because all I can feel now is a sense of loss.

Alright, some good things have happened here, like meeting Mosera and Junior Lake and working with Badejo and being considered a part of things, even if it was just for a little while. I've learned some things about myself, shed some skins, but all in all, it's been one fucking jail sentence in the sun, like drinking pee with a little plastic umbrella in it.

Been in this cultural prison too long and

now I find I am unrecognizable to myself, a prodigal spirit of my own vices and devices.

I've officially become a third class citizen in a second world country.

Last night, I stood outside and did something I hadn't done in a long time; I stood under a palm tree and listened to that noise the wind makes on the leaves, that rustling that sounds like rain but isn't, a ruffling far above my head, a reminder of one more excruciating ecstatic thing about the world I know but cannot grasp.

April 22, 1998
Diary Of A Postal Worker

They say good luck and bad fortune run together; like thunder and lightning, like a stamp on a letter, you can't have one without the other. There is this local guy I know, and it was his dream to work for the Post Office of the Netherlands Antilles in St. Maarten.

To help protect his identity, let's call him King Stampy.

Stampy got word recently he had been hired by the Postal Service and he was ecstatic.

Then, as bad news will follow good, he

learned that his 45 co-workers at the Philipsburg Post Office decided they would not work inside the building for fear the roof would fall in.

That was two weeks ago, and so far, the roof has not moved. But you never know, and so far, no competent authority has been able to give the workers written assurances the roof is safe. So the postal workers stay out of the building and Stampy has plenty of time on his hands.

In order to keep himself occupied, he's kept a diary of a day in the life of a postal worker on strike.

7:50 a.m. Show up for work, I mean no work. Watch other people go to work, begin to forget what it's like.

8:12 a.m.

Take first of several food and beverage breaks. Find the habit of alfresco dining to be relaxing. I fight impulse to fall asleep.

9:03 a.m. Pick up the latest copy of Roof Digest. Review literature on Post Office Roofs; find the data base sadly lacking.

10:32 a.m. Have first of many brief meetings with shop stewards and fellow workers. Stewards report nothing is new, are still awaiting report, I toy with the idea of walking over to Carnival Village.

11:27 a.m. Receive visits from three Executive Council members who promise to appoint a commission to look into a study to propose a feasibility report concerning the actual report that has already been filed that no one has seen.

11:35 a.m. I scratch off the names of at least three Executive Council members I was planning to vote for. Some of my co-workers shift to other side of the street. Why? To get to the other side.

1:43 p.m. Refreshed after lunch and listening to reports of our situation on various news broadcasts, I begin a letter to my fiancee in Calcutta. I go in to post office to post letter but remember I'm on strike. Catch glimpse of postmaster and nice guy Clive Hodge sitting at a desk, filling out papers and looking sad. Maybe it has something to do with 654 bags of mail waiting to be distributed. Funny, he doesn't seem scared to be sitting under the roof.

2:25 p.m. Snack time. Tip-toe into building to heat up cup of tea. Eye roof suspiciously.

3:27 p.m. For eighth time today I tell tourist that Post Office is closed. They ask me about posting letters in Marigot. I tell them, if you think this is bad, just try the post office in Marigot. At least we don't use barricades.

4:26 p.m. Engage in heated debate with co-workers about whether minister Danny Hassell understands the concept of the post office. We decide he does not.

5 p.m. Say goodbye to fellow postal workers and head to car. Feel empty. Eye letter to fiancee. Decide to drive over to Simpson Bay to open a post office box with Mail Box. Mail letter to fiancee in Calcutta. Think to myself, what postal strike?

November 1997

Old girlfriend Judy told me the other day there was something "angelic" about me. It's not a word I would have chosen, but it sounds nice, especially coming from her. But then Judy has also called me the world's smartest retard, informing me, "you are just almost normal enough to realize you will never be able to be happy. You'll stand outside in the cold, nose pressed to the window wondering what warmth is all about."

Maybe.

I prefer the angelic description. It sounds like someone or something that helps people realize their dreams or calm their nightmares. I pop up, materialize, offer some help or empathy, and then disappear. But I know I'm no angel. I am in fact a ghost in the making, it's been preordained, it's my path, my alternative response to ever having been born into the wrong world.

Tenderness and awe, 5758
October 1997

Happy Jewish New Year 5758. Jenny Li and I venture down to Curaçao, the capital of the Netherlands Antilles, to attend services at the oldest synagogue in the western hemisphere. Part of it is a writing assignment for the Guardian, to get more "live" copy from Curaçao into the St. Maarten news, but another part is more atavistic, dare I say spiritual in nature.

From out of the Diaspora, we gather, we Jews, even those like me who view religion like a wrestling match with God, the devil or ourselves, or as a skin graft that will not take.

It's not so much whether or not I believe in god, because in many ways religion and its better cousin, spirituality, have more to do with the living around you than the inanimate and allegorical above you. That's my problem, I have no interest in joining a community of believers. What budding nihilist would?

But something strange happens to me tonight. My pride in being a Jew, a descendant of slaves and Holocaust victims, too often dormant and cloaked in arrogant rage is almost profound and peaceful tonight. Maybe it's the sand underneath my feet, which reminds me Jews have been in transit forever. Cast out of one place, waiting to leave another; never really too comfortable, fleeing prejudice at best, and annihilation at worst.

Maybe it's the beautiful architecture of the synagogue with its burnished wood, or perhaps this is just a night in which spirits are conjured, but I am somehow unhinged, thrown off my cynical balance — moved, and inside me, for a second, even among the whiff of mortality and desperation that surrounds us as Jews, I feel an angelic jolt, Coltrane's "A Love Supreme," a bit of ecstasy I will allow myself to acknowledge.

These are days of tenderness and awe, says the cantor, and I look out the mahogany framed window at a sky gone deep Curaçao blue and watch characters from a Chagall painting float above my head and disappear into breathless clouds fluttering above the Caribbean night.

Lamentations of an Icarus

I have flown too close to the sun
my father did not tell me
that my black licorice wings would melt
a sticky and sickly feeling
the earth rushing to crush me.
I have flown too close to the sun
and I am going to die
but my,
what a tan

Going, going, gone
January 1999

Part of me wishes I could hang around for the Guardian's tenth anniversary in February, but it's not in the cards. Too bad about the Guardian. As much as I can muster any real authentic pity, it's tough to see the paper go down and so far at that. Never could blame my friend Fabian Badejo, even though he probably was not much of a manager. Thing is, he's a decent guy, and he treated me well and with respect. The problem probably resides in the triangulation of Badejo, Joe Dominique and rich man Richard Gibson, who holds all the cards.

Anyway the paper is in trouble, make that slow death, and it pains me to see the awful Herald becoming the paper of record, but hey, what can you do. This is St. Maarten and the lower the common denominator, the better. How else can you explain the success of the Herald, or for that matter morning radio hosts Buzz and the Bulldog, Lloyd Richardson, pimp Sweet Leroy and the empty suits and rah rahs like Eugene Holiday, Terry Gumbs and Liesa Euton who are the regular suspects when some agency or board that never does anything requires another member.

It's very easy to blame things on the pervasive zombiness of St. Maarten, but the bottom line is that it's the Guardian's fault. The paper lost sense of its mission and didn't keep pace with technology. It got to the point where virtually every piece of equipment at the newspaper was broken. It was so bad, we didn't even have proper Internet hook-ups or access to the Associated Press.

For a long time Joe and Badejo have been telling staff the Guardian has more than $500,000 in unpaid collectibles "on the road" but securing even a portion of that money on St. Maarten has proven to be excruciatingly difficult.

Badejo who will also be gone soon, never listened to advice, good suggestions and never saw the future coming. He was spending too much time with Sekou and Junior Lake trying to become a St. Maartener. But he was also burned out from working too long at the paper, it was all on his back for so long, 16 hours a day, six days a week. I cannot blame him for shrugging it off and getting free.

No matter how badly this scene deteriorates, I could never write anything bad about Mr. B. He gave me freedom to write what I wanted, and watched my back. I think he treated me with respect. I'll always like the guy. I'll always remember working with him in the Guardian office, listening to Eddie Williams read the 6 p.m. news and talking trash, always talking trash and laughing his great big Nigerian laugh.

Gibson, the owner of all things Babylon—Burger Kings, a bank, a law firm— just choked the thing to death once it became apparent management had failed to manage. I watch Joe Dominique try and hold the paper together and realize it's all bullshit, that if they wanted it to succeed they would have invested in it and made it work. They wouldn't have wasted time and money on people like the apostle Abigail Richardson who everybody knows was fucking guys for money, hustling, or just plain stealing. She ripped them off regularly while never working, at least not outside of bed. Unlike some others, Abigail always winds up on her back, um, I mean her feet.

I'm not blameless either. In fact, I could be most culpable. I stopped caring a long time ago. I haven't been objective in years, so in essence, I haven't been a real journalist in a long time. I've become intensely negative, vindictive; shrill and hypocritical. Too many people are on my shit list, and I'm on too many of theirs. I probably hurt the paper by being controversial and confrontational on an island that tolerates neither. However you slice it, it's over.

The way I feel now, despite my real affection for Esther and others there, is that it's just one more thing to walk away from, one more bit of evidence that things around me are dying and that if I don't get out of here soon, I will too.

Last Stop
Reprinted from the St. Maarten Guardian, January 29, 1999

When I was a New York City boy, I used to love riding the subway, sometimes all night, taking the "A" train from Washington Heights far out into Brooklyn and Far Rockaway.

Just me and the night crews; the nodding junkies, exhausted hospital orderlies, and the urban vampires dissolving into the metropolitan blackness; urine-soaked, crushed copies of the Daily News and New York Post beneath our feet, the subway cars chugging a steady chunky Samba.

There was always a vague disappointment, an anti-climax, when the train reached its final stop and had to retrace its tracks in the night of morning, leaving the salty ocean air hanging in the subway car as it headed inexorably to another stop.

In New York, one learns early that all rides end, and so, this is my stop.

Before the conductor interrupts us and it gets too noisy to be heard, I'd like to express my affection and appreciation to my friend and boss Fabian Badejo whose loyalty, warmth, intelligence and great laugh I will always remember fondly.

Same too for my colleague Esther Bradshaw-Gumbs; my little sister of the soul, it is as if the soil gives you life and the sky remains your blanket. Esther, whose face sometimes fills with clouds — don't hide from the rain, stay pure. Remember, creativity finds its soul when it embraces its shadow. To the brother like no other, Ras Mosera, my regal friend searching for his stolen blue breadfruit, I just wanted to thank you for all the Friday afternoons, the music of ideas, the multitude of who you are, not to mention the fun. We may not have parted the Caribbean sea, or even the Salt Pond, but we have at last built a bridge. Knowing you makes me feel like a sweepstakes winner.

In just a few weeks the Guardian will celebrate its 10th anniversary, I wish the entire family much luck.

I am grateful to Fabian Badejo and Joe Dominique for the editorial freedom allowed me. At its best under Badejo, the Guardian was the social conscience and voice of independence on St. Maarten.

The level of writing, insight and soul displayed in the Guardian, its courageous and elegant editorials, and the paper's stance against any and all forms of oppression and racism, will never be equaled, no matter how much money KABNA, Hushang Ansari, Reinier Heere, Glen Carty or other entities pour into their respective publications or radio stations.

Badejo, Guardian publisher Richard Gibson, and Dominique created the concept of the community newspaper on St. Maarten and should be proud of it.

Though the product has become inconsistent and suffered, and though management is handcuffed, the paper's soul could be rejuvenated in a new Guardian newspaper, and distance itself from the useless partisan posturing, mediocrity, colonialism and hypocrisy around it. Aim high, provide a lexicon for those struggling with the vocabulary of the times. Take a chance and become the true alternative paper for those sick of the status quo. What's left to lose?

In his famous letter "De Profundus" which was written in prison, the brilliant Oscar Wilde, whose career was marked by arch cleverness and irreverence — he is responsible for the quote, " you must find the thing you like and let it kill you", stripped himself bare emotionally when he wrote, "The final mystery is oneself. When one has weighed the sun in the balance, and measured the steps of the moon, and mapped out the stars, there still remains oneself. Who can calculate the orbit of one's own soul?"

In my orbit in this place I have flirted with disaster, the absurd, elation, divorce, human contact, love, hate,depression, and insensitivity. I watched Roy Cannegieter die slowly before my eyes, and could not prevent it. It was like a long silent scream.

I've been shocked at my own capacity for meanness, duplicity and pettiness, frustrated by caring too much and by not caring at all. I've seen the moment of my mortality come and flicker, seen the eternal footman hold my coat and snicker, and in short, I now know nothing for certain.

Except that it is time to go. Enough? Enough.

"Excuse me, while I disappear"
Frank Sinatra

Recently

Mosera was telling me how he and his wife had been discussing the notion that the Caribbean, as a region, needed some kind of therapy. "A lot of the islands weren't ready, coming out of a post-slavery, post-colonial period and into a culture of poverty," Mosera says.

This is true in St. Maarten where the Dutch, with their clumsy paternalistic "we know best" interpretation of colonial oppression, have no real cultural legacy, no education system as on the British Caribbean Islands, and no hope.

They've always been into money and continue to be. Avarice, Heineken beer and stilted English are the only things they have passed on to their colonial subjects.

The Caribbean, especially St. Maarten needs something, and it needs it fast, before the entire region is consumed by development, tourism and its crushing ignorance and sense of self-importance. Fuck all of them.

As for therapy, let the boiled fish-eating, bullfoot-stew-sipping, teeth-sucking afflicted St. Maarteners breathe Prozac-laced air here on St. Maarten, let them listen to relaxation tapes and get in touch with their collective inner children. Let them kill a couple of tourists per day, let them kill each other, it might be therapeutic.

Or maybe shock treatment. Just hook the whole place up to a huge transformer and give it 50,000 volts, watch all of them spark up like the world's biggest halogen light bulb.

I'm gone now, and I don't care. I've exhausted my unearthly quota of white guilt and acrobatic apologies. Except for Mosera and about five other people, what happens is none of my business anymore.

I do think a lot about Mosera. It's obviously different for him, maybe even poignant. I think he has a real vision of Caribbean integration, of wanting to make things better, and to find a rightful place for himself as a man.

Mosera wants to be at the forefront of something special. Maybe in some other more graceful and generous place it might have worked. Who knows, he may yet be a St. Lucian Moses, and barring forty more years of stumbling in the unreceptive wilderness which is St. Maarten and/or being turned into a pillar of salt, he may find his place, but I know there's no promised land in St. Maarten. You don't have to be Moses, Lot, or Lot's wife to figure that out.

Me? I've got places to go and people to alienate. I can't wait to erase my own life fast enough. I'm feeling more and more that I'm that Siberian tiger my grandpa used to tell me about, a furtive and secretive nomad; a bushy-tailed big cat that erases his own ghost steps in the snow as he walks, so no one can say truly, for sure, that they've seen him.

I was never here.

ABOUT THE AUTHOR

Andy Gross was born in New York City to poor Haitian parents. He was kidnapped by Gypsies at a young age— not a bad thing necessarily, and grew up to attend an Ivy League school.

Andy Gross is a fictional character created by Andrew M. Gross, with whom he enjoys an "on again, off again" relationship. He spent much of the 1980's under house arrest, his own, and did his best to dramatize Franz Kafka's The Hunger Artist.

After his release, Andy Gross assumed the role of journalist in many interesting parts of the United States and the Caribbean where he perfected the art of alienation.

He now resides somewhere not in the Caribbean where he is employed as an apostrophe, always ready to take the place of something, but never the thing itself.

GLOSSARY

Antillean—As used in St. Maarten, this term applies to anyone from the five islands of the Netherlands Antilles, Dutch colonies comprised of Curacao, St. Maarten, Bonaire, St. Eustatius and Saba.

Anguilla— A long, narrow island about seven miles off the coast of St. Martin. Anguilla is a British Dependent Territory.

Axum— A meeting place/ art cafe founded by Ras Mosera and four others in 1997. Mosera came up with the name after reading about a thriving kingdom in Ethiopia circa 500 A.D. that was the nexus for trade between African and Arabian societies until about 750 AD.

The art cafe concept, popular at first ran into hard times after the facility was mismanaged and threatened with legal action and ultimately forced to close its doors.

Four of the original founders, all Babylon Antilleans who I won't name, either left, were forced out, or bailed out when they made no attempt to repay loans or to work out repayment schemes with creditors.

Also, there were a number of creative clashes among the Antillean four and Mosera. It seems an inveterate part of being from or of St. Maarten is to possess a built-in inability to discern quality or to be gracious.

Mosera, now working solo, is trying to restore some of its original luster and still hopes to do some "empire building" of his own.

Babylon—Not just a Rasta or Biblical term, but a state of being— the wicked kingdom of the concrete and poetically challenged; the greedy soul killers, and graceless social climbers and petty slavers who reside here live their literal lives fat with smug entitlement, unaware of the fires burning around them. In short, Babylon is the whole rotten system including police, politicians, phonies and all things polyester.

Bawnhere— Phonetic pronunciation of the words "born here," a term denoting that one was born on St. Maarten and thus entitled to privileges and special treatment that have nothing to do with merit and everything to do with the geopraphy of perception.

Callaloo— The green leaf of the dasheen plant whose root is the noble taro. Dasheen roots and leaves were brought to the new world from West Africa. The leafy vegetable is often served in a spicy West Indian stew.

Colombier— A small village in St. Martin between Marigot and Grand Case. Considered to be among the most verdant and traditionally Caribbean villages still remaining on either side of the island.

Curaçao— The largest of the Netherlands Antilles and the cultural and political center of the five islands. In recent years, there has been much animosity and griping in St. Maarten about island revenues being sent to Curaçao and used in Curaçao, with precious little circling back, largely because Curacao is all but broke and getting broker all the time.

The capital is Willemstad, a beautiful and lively city.

The Daily Herald— Widely read yet terrible newspaper published by colonialist Roger Snow and his immediate family. The paper is not only a mouthpiece for the Dutch government, it is also a refuge for those who are quality challenged, suffer from religious delusions, and those who see no problem in the daily mutilation of syntax and sense.

Democratic Party (DP)— The St. Maarten DP was founded more than forty years ago by drinking buddies Claude Wathey and Clem Labega. Except for the odd term when they weren't in control of the island government and in the role of opposition, the party has ruled St. Maarten for much of this half century and has set unmatchable standards for buying votes with whatever currency might be needed, whether it be cash, stoves, houses or worse. The party has faced numerous allegations of corruption, conflicts of interest and overt malfeasance.

A huge scandal that began more than a decade ago, and a subsequent trial stemming from alleged fraud and perjury charges in connection with St. Maarten's efforts to secure loans from Italian banks to finance the expansion of the Great Bay Harbor and the Princess Juliana International airport, resulted in party co-founder Claude Wathey's fall from power and grace and eventual conviction. Claude Wathey, in declining health, served no jail time, but his son Al, former airport manager Frank Arnell and former Lt. Gov. Ralph Richardson all served jail time.

French Quarter—A traditional Caribbean village in St. Martin that is home to perhaps the worst drivers on the island and the notorious Brooks family.

Frontstreet— The main shopping thoroughfare in Philipsburg, St. Maarten's capital city. Frontstreet runs along the fringe of the Great Bay harbor, and is often clogged by anyone and everyone trying to make a buck, sell a timeshare or looking to buy three T-shirts for $10 for auntie Faye and/or the posse back in New Jersey.

GEBE— The water and power company "serving" St. Maarten. This operation is plagued by numerous problems and spent generators leading to blackouts. The favored explanation for many power outages is that seaweed gets caught in the turbines, or combines or Columbines or whatever, and then, kaput, lights out. The best explanation, I mean excuse, GEBE ever came up with was when they announced a six-hour blackout had been caused by a pesky rat who decided to die inside one of their generators.

Grand Case— A beautiful village in St. Martin that features a great basketball court set against a dramatic backdrop of the mountains on one side and the sparkling sea on the other.
KABNA— The local (St. Maarten) office of the Dutch kingdom government. A vital funding and policy arm of the Colonial government.

Laser 101—A radio station owned by Glen Carty. For more about Glen, I refer you to "Babylon."

Marigot— The de facto capital and commercial center of St. Martin.

Mas— Short for masquerade, a Trinidadian term used to describe the annual celebration of Carnival. "Playing mas" is a big cultural event for most Caribbean islands. St. Maarten's two weeks of Carnival is in mid-April. St. Martin's Carnival coincides with the French observance of Mardi Gras and is held in February.

Mr. Chairman—The formal term used by St. Maarten Island Council members when addressing the lieutenant governor, who is the chairman of the Island Council and a direct appointee of the Dutch Kingdom government. The lieutenant governor, who is the local police chief and head of the election board and who enjoys wide and sweeping powers as delineated by the Dutch government, is ostensibly neutral, but this is never the case. Former lieutenant governors Ralph Richardson and Russell Voges were decidedly in line with the Democratic Party, while current Lt. Gov. Dennis Richardson is considered sympathetic toward the St. Maarten Patriotic Alliance.

PJD2— The most powerful radio station on the island, broadcasting out of Philipsburg.

Pondfill— St. Maarten's official garbage dump which grows more imposing and disgusting year after year. Situated beside what was once a lovely salt water pond, the Pondfill is both an eyesore and a health hazard. When the wind is just right, or in this case, wrong, the stench from the Pondfill is nauseating and is a tourist and resident nightmare.

Rollocks, Julian— The founder of the Serious Alternative Peoples Party. otherwise known as the SAPP. Rollocks, known at the Guardian as "King Home Alone", began his career trying to operate outside the system by stressing his "bread and butter" issues. It might have worked, but Hurricane Luis and Rollock's own ambition got in the way. Once he got in office, bread and butter gave way to croissants and caviar.

St. Martin/St. Maarten —Located about 170 miles from Puerto Rico, and lightyears from god, this 35 square-mile island is home to two separate entities, the French Overseas Territory of St. Martin, and the Dutch Colony of St. Maarten. St. Martin is an actual department of France, and St. Martiners can vote in national elections. St. Maarteners can only vote for themselves in what Joe Lake Jr. calls their little "dollhouse" elections. They have no say in anything, yet they never stop talking.

St. Martin, which is the northern part of the island is roughly 21 square-miles and is in danger of being completely overrun by the French, which is leading to quite a bit of tension with the gradually diminishing native St. Martiners.

The island was discovered by the Spanish in the early 16th century but was not settled, according to the Caribbean Companion.

In 1648, French and Dutch settlers, who had arrived nearly 20 years earlier, divided the island between them and the boundaries remain in effect today. The island has open borders which makes travel as well as crime commission a relatively simple matter.

The Princess Juliana International Airport is in Dutch St. Maarten, but that's just a formality, because most people who come to St. Maarten now come by cruise ship. Most air arrivals either head straight to the French north side of the island, or simply transfer at the airport for flights to Anguilla and St. Barts, now considered more upscale destinations.

Printed in the United States
20195LVS00001B/82

9 781930 859012